TALES OF
OKINAWA'S
GREAT
MASTERS

BY

SHOSHIN NAGAMINE

TRANSLATED BY

PATRICK MCCARTHY

Tuttle Publishing
Boston • Rutland, Vermont • Tokyo

First published in 2000 by Tuttle Publishing,
an imprint of Periplus Editions (HK) Ltd., with editorial offices at
153 Milk Street, Boston, Massachusetts 02109.

Library of Congress Cataloging-in-Publication Data in process
ISBN: 0-8048-2089-9

Distributed by

USA
Tuttle Publishing
Distribution Center
Airport Industrial Park
364 Innovation Drive
North Clarendon, VT 05759-9436
Tel: (800) 526-2778
Tel: (802) 773-8930

SOUTHEAST ASIA
Berkeley Books Pte. Ltd.
5 Little Road #08-01
Singapore 536983
Tel: (65) 280-3320
Fax: (65) 280-6290

JAPAN
Tuttle Publishing
RK Building, 2nd floor
2-13-10 Shimo-Meguro Meguro-Ku
Tokyo 153-0064
Tel: (03) 5437-0171
Fax: (03) 5437-0755

CANADA
Raincoast Books
8680 Cambie Street
Vancouver, Canada V6P 6M9
Tel: (604) 323-7100
Fax: (604) 323-2600

First edition
05 04 03 02 01 00   1 3 5 7 9 10 8 6 4 2
Printed in the United States of America

**Commemorative photograph of Shoshin Nagamine taken
in 1982 upon his receipt of the Fifth Class Order of the
Rising Sun from the Emperor of Japan. Nagamine was 75
at the time.**

Acknowledgments

I deeply appreciate the many people who have assisted me with the research for this modest publication: Kikuzato Kyobun of Kumejima; Kinjo Setsu of Motobu village; Nakasone Seishin of the Toguchi Police Department; Tamashiro Rinzo and Nagahama Zansho of the Heian-za; Ishizuka Itoku and Tomoyose Eigen of Naha. I am grateful to Patrick and Yuriko McCarthy who spent nearly one year translating this book into English. Charles C. Goodin of Hawaii proofread and provided technical assistance with the English text. I am also indebted to the many other people whose important contributions helped make this book a great success.

Table of Contents

I wonder if it was 1940 or 1941 that I first noticed that remarkable photograph in the display corner of Matayoshi's Photo Studio on Uenokura Street in Naha. It was a photograph portraying two men standing together, bare-chested. Their musculature was very impressive. One man wore a topknot, and at a glance I could tell he was a sumo wrestler. By comparison, the other man was very short and narrow-shouldered. However, his deeply trained muscles and bone structure were not inferior to that of the six-foot sumo wrestler.

At that time I had come home to Okinawa for winter vacation, but I remember returning to Tokyo with an impression of that picture still fresh in my mind. Fortunately I had a friend, a sturdy *shodan* (1st degree black belt) in judo, who also practiced karate, from whom I found out more about that impressive photograph.

The sumo wrestler was named Satonishiki and the other man was Mr. Nagamine Shoshin, a local master of karate. My friend explained that Nagamine Sensei was a policeman and one of the most prominent martial artists in Okinawa. Although this was my first time to hear the name of Nagamine Shoshin I already knew of his physique from the photo at Matayoshi's studio. I also learned that the sumo wrestler Satonishiki was ranked in the top ten by the monthly magazine *Baseball World*. At that time, headline articles and pictorials of sumo wrestlers were featured in this popular magazine, issued by Baseball Magazine Company.

The physical contrast between Nagamine Shoshin and Satonishiki was obvious from that photo. However, being neither an expert of physical education nor familiar with karate or sumo, I was uncertain who was the stronger of the two. Admiring that photograph at the Matayoshi Photo studio, I still remember to this day how impressed I was by it.

The eminent Funakoshi Gichin came from the head of my family. He was the cousin of my father. Gichin's father's name was Gishu, and my grandfather, Gifu, was his brother. Actually, Funakoshi Gichin was old enough to be the parent of my father. Funakoshi Gichin's second son, Giyu, was the same age as my father. In my youth I was influenced by uncle Giyu, and often visited Gichin's house. At that time he had his new dojo at the Kishimojin area in Zoshigaya, Tokyo.

Called the Shotokan, I often visited Funakoshi's dojo on Sundays as a messenger of uncle Giyu. Uncle Gigo, the third son of Funakoshi Gichin, taught there at that time. Uncle Gigo commanded me to practice in the dojo, but Gichin Sensei said I was not suited to practice karate. That didn't mean that I was not interested in karate, it just meant that I didn't practice it. However, I continued going to the dojo regularly. I wanted to be strong like other boys, but the notion of training my mind and spirit through the discipline of martial arts just did not capture me at that time. However, I now regret that I could not find the courage to enter Gichin Sensei's world, even though I was so close to him.

It was Nagamine Ichiro (no relation) who first gave me the chance to feel close to Nagamine Shoshin Sensei. Nagamine Ichiro had asthma as a child. However, after he studied karate under Nagamine Sensei, his health improved. After the war, Nagamine Ichiro recommended that I also consider practicing karate because of my asthma problem. At that time, both Ichiro and I worked for the Okinawan Peoples' Government (forerunner of the Ryukyu government). Ichiro had overcome his asthma problem through karate training. This interested me, but I couldn't decided whether or not to begin training because I was so lazy.

Even though I had heard the name of Nagamine Shoshin often since 1940 or 1941, it was not until I moved back to Naha in 1950 that I was finally able to meet him. I can't remember just how I became so close to Nagamine Sensei, but I did.

These days I don't see Nagamine Sensei very often, but when I do, I feel as if it was just yesterday that we last met. That's how close we are. Yet, not being a *budoka,* I can't imagine that I am a very good companion for the master, never speaking about the discipline. Nonetheless, the story of Master Nagamine's enlightenment through *bu* is a great lesson for us all. Master Nagamine is a great inspiration, not only for *karateka,* but also for people like myself, who remain outside of the discipline.

In this book, Master Nagamine presents the combat legacy of our people: the legend of Okinawa's *bushi* (warriors). Included in his presentation are Matsumura of Shuri, Matsumora of Tomari, Motobu Saru, and Kyan Chotoku, among others, all famous *bujin* (martial artists). After I read the manuscript once, I felt that this was the first book about karate that was both illuminating and easy to understand.

I was impressed that Nagamine Sensei did not introduce karate in a mysterious way, as if it was an obscure or "all-mighty" phenomenon. Rather, the art has been presented by a person who knows karate very well, a person who truly understands the real meaning of the discipline and its authentic *waza* (technique). Mysterious stories about karate sometimes confuse the actual purpose of the art. I can understand and accept the reason behind them, as they serve to spark interest in young boys. However, each reader or listener should interpret the message in his own way.

Stories about courageous warriors have always provided young boys with dreams about becoming strong and moral. Since karate-do is native to our island, it provides a sense of patriotism and regard for one's heritage and community. I too, remember as an elementary student reading a story which left a remarkable impression on me. So too, I believe, will Nagamine Shoshin's impressive publication greatly influence the young people of this generation.

Even though I know little about karate-do, I still maintain a great passion for this remarkable tradition. Every time I have observed a demonstration of the art by young people, I have been moved. When I see the frightening beauty of karate's magnificent ferocity I experience an inner exhilaration. Strange as it may seem, I secretly shed a tear of regret for the great opportunity I had let pass.

Nearly a half-century has passed since I first saw the photograph of Nagamine Sensei and Satonishiki. Yet, still full of life, it is as if Nagamine just stepped out of the photograph yesterday. Having contributed so much to the growth and development of karate-do in Okinawa and throughout the world, we are all deeply grateful for Nagamine Sensei's outstanding efforts, and this book is a testament to his dedication.

—Funakoshi Gisho

I would like to say that this book is interesting, and I am impressed to say the very least. The reason I found it interesting was because it was written by someone who, as a modern *bushi* himself, was able to convincingly portray the legacy of Okinawa's old *bushi*.

Before reading this book I had no idea that the *bushi* and the arts shared any connection. Moreover, and in all modesty, I also have to say that I had no real knowledge of Bushi Nagamine Shoshin either. However, after having read his book, twice, I came to understand much more than I had ever expected.

Historically, there have always been misunderstandings surrounding karate masters and Okinawan sumo wrestlers alike. Oral tradition characterizes them as hero-like figures, and television dramas portray them as such. However, the more I read Nagamine Sensei's book, the more I had to modify my preconception. After first reading Funakoshi Gisho's foreword, I thought it was a little exaggerated, and chalked it up to supporting the author. However, after carefully reading the subsequent pages, I came to realize two important facts: the detailed explanation of *bunbu,* and the documentation which Nagamine Sensei had compiled from his extensive research and interviews.

I was also impressed that Nagamine Sensei had carefully corroborated his historical investigation with either the testimonies of the masters themselves or their immediate families. Additionally, Nagamine Sensei's superb writing forte is second only to his deep understanding of karate-do which is clearly evident in the way this book has been composed. This publication should therefore represent a scale by which to measure the depth of a man who devoted his entire life to karate-do.

I am not a person who easily expresses my feelings; however, when reading a stirring book, and especially if I am moved, tears often culminate my emotions. For this, my family has often teased me. Yet, I experienced the same feeling when reading this book. My family laughed at me, but that did nothing to change the way I felt. I was truly touched.

In this fascinating book, historical inaccuracies surrounding Okinawan martial folklore have been corrected. Hence, we can read stories about stalwarts like Makabe Choken, To-Te Sakugawa Kanga, Matsumura Sokon, Matsumora Kosaku, Itosu Anko, Higaonna Kanryo, Funakoshi Gichin, Kyan Chotoku, Motobu Choki, and Arakaki Ankichi.

This book also describes the training chronicles of Okinawa's sumo community. For example, it recounts the stories of Akarie Matsuzo, Kawamae Kitatsu, Kinjo Masayuki, Uezu Jiryo, and Ishikawa Seijin. Moreover, this fascinating publication also introduces Kushi Jokei, who, by all accounts, enjoyed a glorious interval as a post-war leader of the sumo community in Okinawa.

As I stated at the beginning of this foreword, this book is an interesting publication in that it represents an authentic account of pre- to post-war Okinawan karate masters, *bujin,* and native sumo wrestlers, their bouts and reputations. Most of all, these chronicles are introduced by Nagamine Shoshin, a master of *bunbu ryo do:* someone whose physical skills are equally balanced by his intellectual dexterity.

As mentioned earlier, at first I thought Funakoshi Gisho's foreword was exaggerated. However, after reading the manuscript, I concur. This book is a must for everyone who studies karate. Moreover, I also recommend it as a source from which the modern *bujin* can better understand karate and Zen, as well as knowing karate's place in Okinawan culture.

—Kadekawa Junki
Journalist, *Ryukyu Shinpo*
[Note: This foreword first appeared in the *Ryukyu Shinpo* evening
edition on July 12th, 1986.]

It is both an honor and a surprise that I should be associated with Grandmaster Nagamine's book. First, it is a honor that someone as important as Nagamine Shoshin considered me worthy to undertake the translation of such important research. Second, it is ironic because the very first book on the history of karate-do I ever bought, more than twenty years ago, was Professor Shinzato Katsuhiko's wonderful English translation of O-Sensei's first publication, *The Essence of Okinawan Karate-Do.* Having made a big impression on me, I never thought that I would one day befriend such a man, much less be petitioned to translate his research, and then write a foreword for its publication. It just proves that anything is possible.

I first met the great master during my pilgrimage to Okinawa in the summer of 1985. Living in Japan, I have personally enjoyed many training opportunities with O-Sensei in the years which have since past. To learn from a master, who had himself been taught by such legendary figures as Motobu Choki, Kyan Chotoku, and Arakaki Ankichi, has been a privilege which words can hardly describe.

During my lengthy analysis and English translation of Okinawa's enigmatic book, *Bubishi,* I was fortunate to obtain the assistance of Grandmaster Nagamine. It was during that time that I really got to know more about Nagamine Shoshin the man, and the principles for which he stands. It is no secret that his guidance has had a profound impact on the way I embrace karate-do, in the way I assess its evolution, its value to society, and my personal philosophy with regard to its future direction.

Every generation produces experts who, in an effort to keep their tradition a living experience for the society it serves, reinterpret the common principles on which it rests. Nagamine Shoshin is one such man, and this book is a testament to his incomparable research, profound knowledge, and commendable dedication. If I have gained any further insight into karate-do, its history, philosophy, and application, then it has been because of men like *bushi* Nagamine Shoshin. He is the most senior authority of karate-do in the world today. I highly recommend this book to both teacher and student alike.

—Patrick McCarthy
Director, International Ryukyu Karate Research Society

It was February of 1975 that my modest book, *Okinawan Karate-do: The Preservation of a Traditional Legacy,* was first published by Shinjinbutsuorai-sha in Tokyo. Much to my surprise the book met with such popularity that I was asked to have it translated into English, a task completed by Professor Shinzato Katsuhiko. The English version was published and released in October of the same year by the Charles E. Tuttle Publishing Company under the new title *The Essence of Okinawan Karate-do.* I received many letters of encouragement from karate enthusiasts from all over the world.

Many of the letters asked me if I would consider writing about the lives of Okinawa's old *bujin.*

Shoshin Nagamine

This, coupled with similar requests I had received over the years from both students and colleagues, prompted me to think seriously about such a project. Most of the historical documentation about such men is believed to be greatly embellished and uncorroborated. Examples of such things include stalwarts able to swing their way across the beams of a ceiling using only the fingertips; men able to, with a single blow, rip the flesh from the body of a living ox; a tiny man able to kick a barrel full of sugar up onto a cart with only his foot; and karate men able to splinter jumbo stalks of green bamboo by simply seizing them by hand.

Tales such as these are, at best, difficult to believe and cast doubt on the art. Moreover, the storytellers are themselves usually old men who either briefly learned karate in their youth, or never learned it at all! Having observed an impressive demonstration a long time ago, the feats tend to gain something each time the story is told. Long-winded old men often recount stories as if they had actually happened. This, unfortunately, has resulted in listeners misunderstanding the true value of karate-do. With this in mind, I believe that my first book has prompted many people, both at home and abroad, to petition me to describe the actual historical events, personalities, and abilities of Okinawa's old *bujin*.

From 1969 to 1983 I travelled four times to Canada, the United States, Argentina, and Uruguay to teach and lecture on karate-do, its history, philosophy, and application. By doing so, I was able to strengthen Matsubayashi-ryu karate-do and expand the World Matsubayashi-ryu (Shorin-ryu) Karate-Do Association. Cradled in our tiny island, haphazardly enhanced by Chinese *chuan fa,* and then further cultivated before being introduced, and reinterpreted again, on the mainland of Japan, karate-do has enjoyed a fascinating evolution. In spite of the modern karate movement which started a mere half-century ago, karate-do has now found its way to the four corners of the world. When compared with Japan's other cultural combative disciplines, karate-do has achieved a world-wide popularity which kendo, judo, or ever sumo has yet to realize. In all honesty, even having been a part of the pioneering process, I can hardly believe the magnitude by which karate-do has grown.

When I am asked about Okinawa, I often like to say that it is the island from which karate first surfaced, rather than describing it as the location that was decimated during the Second World War. I feel confident that most foreigners whom I have met are satisfied with my description. Yet, a question which remains unanswered is how karate achieved such international magnitude?

Considering its practical attributes, the ability "to kill with a single blow" or similar "supernatural powers of destruction," were developed by learning to use the entire body as a weapon. It is not surprising, then, that such a practice spread so rapidly. However, the principal basis for karate's world-wide popularity has to be the "anytime, anywhere, anyone" principle. Simply put, the practice of karate knows no limitations; there are no time, place, age, or gender restrictions.

One can train any time, any place, and with anyone, or even by one-self. Moreover, one can practice for fitness, self-defense, recreation, competition, character development, or spiritual discovery. Especially in such a hectic modern society as ours, karate is an attractive and practical consideration.

In spite of this enormous popularity, we must not lose sight of that which the competitive element and commercial exploitation have generated. Ignorance and misunderstanding have fueled eclecticism in countries whose cultures are unlike that from which karate evolved. As such, karate has been popularized for its utilitarian and competitive elements and, for the most part, monopolized by young people. In so doing, the classical values on which the art rests have been ignored. Karate is a tradition which should be practiced by both young and old, male and female, and *kata* is the central vehicle of this profound discipline. I believe that without restoration of these values, true classical Okinawan karate will become extinct.

I do not mean to suggest that I have a totally negative opinion of karate's competitive dimension, it is just that I feel it is too shallow. Regardless of whether it is in Okinawa, the mainland of Japan, or the world in general, *jyu-kumite* (free-sparring) ignores the principles on which *kata* is based. Simply put, *jyu-kumite* should in some way reflect *kata,* because *kata* is the origin of karate. If there is no *kata,* there is no karate, just kicking and punching.

Respecting the fact that *kata* is karate, one must embrace the *dō mu gen* proverb, which, simply stated, asserts: "There can be no end to learning." Hence, karate begins and ends with the study of *kata.* *Kata* is the way through which the secrets of karate have been transmitted from the beginning. Moreover, the only way in which karate can be effectively handed down to future generations as a cultural inheritance, is by adhering to this tradition.

When I think about the international exposure which karate-do has received, I can not help but ponder the footsteps of our eminent predecessors and the devotion it took to forge this tradition. In spite of nearly three centuries of harsh living in the shadows of foreign military and political subjugation, our predecessors never lost their lively spirit. One notable aristocrat named Tansui Eekata (1623–82) composed an abstract poem which has become a classic among Ryukyu folk art.

Poem:
    Chunomiya muchai   *Ashibushiya warate*
    Kunoyu furishite te   *Ichayashigana*

Translation:
A human life span is like a fleeting drop of dew.
Renounce people who play. Yet, if possible, I wish
to go to Shangri-la.

Clarification:
"Renounce people who play" refers to Tansui Eekata revering music so much that other statesmen criticized his preoccupation and artistic achievements. The word "play," in this case, implies his "taste for music." Hence, Tansui was mistakenly thought to be lethargic, during a period of Okinawan history when men of his position were expected to use their influence and power in more productive ways. After returning from the countryside where he had spent considerable time composing music, he was finally recognized as a great musician, and regarded as the founder of *Tansui-ryu* (Tansui school). In the end, Tansui was considered a creative genius and an overachiever.

In my opinion, Tansui is a perfect example of one who deeply embraces the spirit of *dō mu gen:* there is no end to learning. In spite of adversity and misunderstanding, he devoted his entire life to artistic accomplishment. I was deeply moved with Tansui's *chimugukuru* (devotion).

It was around my second year of junior high school, under the old prewar school system, that I started training in karate. In those days, everyone thought of a *bushi* as someone who was just a strong fighter. Yet, even as a child, I somehow perceived that this opinion was incorrect, and that being a *bushi* meant more than just being physically powerful.

As a lad, I was fortunate to have met a prominent teacher and his great senior disciple. Because of their profound understanding of karate, so too was I able to achieve a deep perception of *budo* (martial ways). In other words, I was able to confirm my childhood beliefs that a *bushi* was more than just a physically powerful person. I came to understand how devoting one's life to karate develops an indomitable spirit and unshakable faith. This is necessary for a *bujin* to live a just life and is similar to Buddhist beliefs.

I became a policeman at the age of twenty-six because it suited me, and I kept enthusiastically practicing judo, kendo, and karate. During that time I often visited prominent senior *bujin,* not really caring whether they were from the Shuri-te or Tomari-te traditions. In addition to enhancing my understanding of karate in general, I also managed to pick up many descriptions of old *bujin* from the Ryukyu Kingdom.

Between 1940 and 1944, I researched the family lineages of Bushi

Matsumura Sokon, Makabe Chaan (Makabe Choken), Mayaa Arakaki (Arakaki Seisho Tsuji) of Naha's Kumemura, and Bushi Matsumora Kosaku of Tomari. After the war I supplemented this analysis by conducting more investigation into corresponding areas. Only then was I able to conclude my examination into the lives and times of those men who grace the pages of the book which lies before you. Together, these men represent some of the most prominent pioneers of karate history.

As I mentioned earlier, the competitive dimension and commercial exploitation have given rise to eclecticism in Okinawa and beyond. Simply stated, this is a departure from authentic Okinawan karate. Other details to consider are the erroneous stories which are mistakenly construed as historical facts. The problem with such embellished stories is that they have gone on unchallenged and have become legends.

In many ways, I feel that it is my responsibility to not only reestablish the authentic image of karate-do, but to also hand down an important piece of Okinawa's cultural legacy. In spite of my inadequate writing skills, I am able to not only give back to the art which has given me so much, but also return my obligation to those *bujin* who have come before me. In doing so, it is my deepest hope that the entire karate community, both here in Okinawa and abroad, may come to understand that which they have yet to learn.

I really appreciate the support of Funakoshi Gisho, Kadekawa Juuki, and all the other kind people who assisted with the research and publication of this book. I would like to especially thank Gakiya Joshu, the calligrapher who brushed the kanji for this book; Miyagi Akira who painted the portraits which appear in this book; and my seniors, Mr. Nagamine Shoshu and Mr. Sakugawa Kankei, who helped me research the family lineages.

Because there is so little official documentation about the old *bujin* of Okinawa's karate history, I have taken this opportunity to make available much of that information which has been handed down through oral tradition. Not really considering myself an expert of karate-do, I would like to say that any and all mistakes which may appear in this book are mine alone.

PART ONE

BIOGRAPHIES OF OKINAWAN KARATE EXPERTS

Chapter 1

MAKABE CHOKEN OKINA:
A MAN OF GREAT STRENGTH

THE DIVINE JUMPING TECHNIQUES OF TOBITORI

There was a hospital owned by Taira Masa which was situated in Shuri's Tounukura district before the war. This was the same site where the Makabe estate once stood. Makabe's residence covered an area of 360 *tsubo* (1188 meters) and many kinds of *budo* training equipment were located there. Makabe Choken Okina is said to have trained there every day. Thanks to the Taira family, I enjoyed the privilege of inspecting a footprint on the ceiling of the guest house, put there, rumor

Portrait of Makabe

maintains, by Makabe himself while demonstrating a jump kick. I went there with the interest of confirming it with my own eyes. Using my eye to compare the height of the ceiling in this old style residence to those of other Okinawan-style homes, I would say that it was over four meters high.

Makabe Choken was born the fourth son of Makabe Aji Chougi (whose Chinese name was Jigenho), during the time of King Shoboku. Choken's childhood name was Umijiru and his Chinese name was Koubunbin. He grew quite large during his youth and by the age of fifteen or sixteen, he developed into an enormous man of muscle.

Coming from a family of wealth and position, Makabe

2

received a good education which, during Okinawa's Ryukyu Kingdom, was referred to as *Teshimi Gakumun: te* means "hand" but implies martial arts, *shimi* means "calligraphy" but implies a scholarly pursuit (i.e., the study of Confucianism), and *gakumun* means "to study." Together, they represent the principles of *bun bu ryo dō:* the significance of balancing physical training with philosophical study. In addition, Makabe also became familiar with Japanese academic pursuits.

In spite of Makabe's well-known reputation as a *bujin,* who trained him and in what tradition remains the subject of intense curiosity. Notwithstanding, it would seem that whoever was responsible for his education did a remarkable job.

Makabe was respected as a talented man, with a good physique and remarkable power. During Makabe's youth there were other strong young men who challenged him. One young stalwart was a man named Funakoshi. Funakoshi had gained a reputation as a brave strong fellow after pinning a fighting bull to the ground by twisting its head and holding it down by the horns.

The confrontation was held on the grounds of the Makabe residence. In preparation for the bout several *shiijakata* (referees) and a horde of excited young men had gathered in the courtyard to observe the exhibition. First the contestants were required to demonstrate their strength by lifting a ninety kilogram *chikarasaashi* (old style stones used in power training, similar to today's barbells). First Makabe, without much effort, did twenty quick presses over his head before putting the apparatus back down on the ground. The audience remained collected as they knew Makabe trained every day. However, when it came time for Funakoshi to attempt the lift there was a pause. He was unfamiliar with the equipment and the conditions were different from what he was used to, and the audience sensed it too. Yet, in spite of the variations, Funakoshi attacked the *chikarasaashi* and rat-

tled off the same amount of repetitions as did Makabe. The crowd was astonished by Funakoshi's power and immediately showed its enthusiasm.

Next came the *chikarabo,* a game which tested the power, balance, and dexterity of its participants. It required each contestant to brace the end of a *bo* on a

Illustration of the *chikarabo* bout.

point just below the umbilicus (the *tanden*) and hold onto it with both hands. Thrusting at each other while keeping the posture in a pliable but authoritative position, victory depends entirely on a keen sense of positioning. Weight and strength are not enough to win. Just like *budo,* knowing the principles of *taisabaki* (body movement), and *kiaijutsu* (the build up, containment, and release of *ki*) had to be mastered in order to overcome any opponent.

Still intact after about an hour or so, the *shiijakata* ordered the contestants to change position. Once again they vigorously went at each other but to no avail. Finally the *shiijakata* declared the bout a draw, it was just too close a game. All but burned out, Makabe and Funakoshi took a rest for a while before starting the next event to settle the contest.

Agreeing to test their *tobigeri* (jumping kicks), the next event finally got under way. The location was changed from the courtyard into the guest house of the Makabe residence.

The guest house of the Taira residence. Photo from the *Ryukyu Kenhoshi.*

Committed from youth to a life of *budo,* Makabe Chaan had more than adequately trained his running and jumping skills. He believed that the essence of combative superiority existed in pliability, not in stationary postures, and Makabe found Mt. Hantan, and Mt. Torazu ideal terrain for strengthening such skills. The Taira family maintained that whenever Makabe returned home late at night, like a *ninja,* he would jump over the stone gate which surrounded the residence so as not to disturb his family. The *umoteyaajou* (front gate) was the symbol of an Okinawan *kemochi* (those with a chronicled lineage; the equivalent of a Japanese samurai family) during the Ryukyu Kingdom period. However, the gate, like so many other treasures of Okinawa, was destroyed during the war.

The gate of the Taira residence. This photo originally appeared in the *Ryukyu Ihoshi.*

Generally speaking, a big man is usually strong but lacks mobility. However, Makabe Chaan was the exception to the rule. Incidentally, the suffix *Chaan* is a term which refers to a small, quick, and brave fighting cock. Hence, this nickname has led many to erroneously believe that Makabe was a small person.

In 1944, Makabe Chosho, a sixth generation descendant of Makabe Chaan, visited me at my request. The owner of a tea business in Naha's Higashi-machi, he was kind enough to provide me with the family genealogy. His assistance was of enormous value to my research. However, my analysis along with his family records were unfortunately destroyed during an air raid on October 10, 1944. I am deeply sorry that I was unable to take better care of the Makabe family records.

Helping to corroborate Makabe Chaan's actual size, Chosho-san recounted a story which I would like to impart. There was a kimono made from *bashofu* (bark from the *bashoo* tree). It was Makabe Chaan's special keepsake from Amami, a principal island in the Ryukyu Archipelago, and was well cared for and handed down in the family. Although Makabe Chosho was an average size man, the kimono was, however, too long for him, even when he stood on the top of thick chess board. Although a minor point, it does, nonetheless, tells us that Makabe Chaan wasn't a small man, as some would have us believe, but was more than six feet tall.

Makabe Chotoku, the vice president of the Ryukyu Fire Insurance Company, is a seventh generation descendant of Makabe Chaan. When Chotoku was rebuilding the family grave site after the war, he inspected Makabe's bones. He said that he was surprised to see that his leg bones were so long. I believe that the information which I received from Taira, Chosho, and Chotoku, would all seem to indicate that Makabe Chaan was indeed of more than just average size.

To continue with the confrontation between Makabe and Funakoshi, there is an abstract poem which I believe characterizes their encounter.

Poem:
  Bushi no miya, sura ni
  tobu toi no kukuchi,
  michimiteinteiniya touiyanaran

Interpretation:
  The movements of a real *bushi* are not unlike those
  of a bird in flight: swift, natural, and without
  thought. Regardless of one's physical strength,
  catching a bird is virtually impossible.

Although Makabe was big and powerful, he was also unusually agile, no doubt the result of his intense training. Seemingly, Funakoshi clung to the idea that power was enough to overcome an opponent. He had successfully stalemated Makabe in the tests of power, and believed that he was ready to challenge the technique of the great *bushi*.

Now came the opportunity for Makabe to test the results of his lengthy training in jumping techniques. He took his stance as he prepared to unleash his kick. Looking calmly up at the ceiling of the guest house Makabe wasted no time springing into position before leaping up, and, with an enormous *kiai* (spirit shout), executing a jump kick as fast, and higher, than anyone in that room had seen before. Landing back on the *tatami* mat, Makabe finished his kicking demonstration in the *meikata* posture (an elegant position used in Okinawan folk dancing to music during village festivals). As the spectators stood in awe, the imprint of Makabe's foot, remaining clearly visible on the ceiling, served to remind everyone of the incredible feat they had just witnessed.

When it came time for Funakoshi to perform, it remained obvious to Makabe that he was flustered. Having never even seen, let alone practiced, a jumping kick, Funakoshi scrambled to learn. Attempting to duplicate that which he had just observed, Funakoshi, in spite of Makabe's friendly advice, fell flat on the back of his head, unconscious. By the time the fallen Funakoshi finally came to, he realized that he had been outmatched and, as was often the case in those days, asked Makabe to become his teacher.

A HEROIC EPISODE

During the Kingdom period, the *ayajou-uugina* (tug of war) was always a spectacular event in the old castle town of Shuri. Supported by the people of Mitara district, and authorized by the *sanshikan* (top three ministers in office), the tug of war was an event held primarily for Okinawa's *kemochi*. The rope used in Naha had a diameter of three *shaku* and each side measured thirty *ken* (54.54 meters) in length, for an overall length of sixty *ken* (109.08 meters). The rope used in Shuri was twice the size of that used in Naha, and measured a magnificent 120 *ken* (218.18 meters) in length.

An event not taken lightly, the tug of war was a contest governed by strict rules. According to *Naha City Magazine,* the tug of war committee consisted of a *buuhai* (head of tug of war), *chinahoo* (maker of the rope), *teehoo* (maker of the lanterns), *shitaakuhoo* (maker of the costumes), *chinkuhoo* (conductor of the music), *kanichihoo* (maker of the wooden *bo*), *suneehoo* (chief of the parade guards), and *hatahoo* (maker and coach of the flags).

As previously explained, the *ayajou-uugina* was a popular cultural event which always attracted a crowd of people ranging from local government and *satsuma* officials, to *kemochi* and *mukei* (those without chronicled lineage). Because it was the most spectacular event in the Ryukyu Kingdom, participation in it was the ambition of all the young men from Shuri's Mitara district. The holding of the flag and the *kanuchiyaku* (the staff) was considered a special honor, customarily a privilege reserved only for brave and bold men. A man selected for one of these roles was considered to be not only a man among men; he was truly revered.

It came as no surprise to learn that, in representing the east, Makabe Chaan was always selected for such positions since he was tall, powerful, and popular. The flag for the west, representing the opposition, was often held by Morishima Eekata, a man of Herculean strength. Morishima later had a son who became known as Giwan Choho, a prominent statesman, who died in 1875.

The tug of war as shown in the *Ryukyu Ihoshi*.

The *shitaku* (costume) for the east was designed after the historical boy samurai Ushiwakamaru (actually Minamoto Yoshitsune's childhood name), while the *shitaku* worn by the west represented Benkei (a subordinate of Yoshitsune's who dressed like a monk). With a first swing of the flag, the tug of war commenced and the ringing of the bells and drums became intense. After a superb *kanuchibo* demonstration, the participants gathered around the rope to engage each other. The grunts and shouts of physical exertion filtered through the music and commotion as an excited throng of spectators swarmed the venue. Yet, in the end, the game belonged to the east. Makabe's team had emerged victorious.

As was the custom, the first and second flagsmen led the winner's side around while the champions rang the bells, beat the drums, screamed feverishly in triumph, and danced around in high spirits. Regulation demanded that the losing team should quietly place the head of their flag on the ground and retreat in defeat.

However, at this particular event the west, representing the *hatahoo* (the vanquished), were

The *hatagashira* (head of the flag).

poor losers and forgot their etiquette. Refusing to surrender their icon, they kept screaming and sailing the defeated flag in an effort to taunt the champions. Just as everyone began to notice what was going on, Makabe jumped into the midst of the defeated team like a flying bird, grabbed the flag and threw it to the ground and then withdrew without recourse. The audience, as well as the other team members, were overwhelmed by his bravery.

In old Okinawa, high ranking *kemochi* often used a palanquin to travel around. Not being immune to the problems of highway robbery, Makabe Chaan was well-known for his innovative techniques of defense and escape. One night there was a palanquin traveling through the dark streets of Shuri. The two palanquin holders suddenly felt apprehensive because the weight of their passenger had mysteriously vanished. When they put the palanquin down to check inside, it was empty. They were dumbfounded. All of a sudden they were overcome by fear as a black shadow jumped out from behind a well by the street. Without delay the two palanquin holders ran off in fear of their lives. Just then a voice yelled out, "Don't be afraid men, come back." Laughing quietly to himself, the voice was that of Makabe Chaan who was supposed to be in the palanquin.

I've heard a similar story from the great master of karate, Motobu Choki. There once was a man named Sakuma Chikudoun Peichin who, by all accounts, was a brave but imprudent fighter. Notwithstanding, Motobu raised his hat to this dauntless stalwart. Apparently Sakuma also liked drinking and often accepted challenges in exchange for *awamori* (a potent Okinawan liquor). Once in Shuri, Sakuma leaped into a *miga* (well) and then came flying out again. He was able to accomplish this feat by pressing his hands and feet against the sides of the well to support his powerful body. Even the powerful Motobu Choki was unable to perform such a magnificent feat.

Sakuma Peichin's remarkable jumping technique was based on the skills of Makabe Chaan. Since boyhood Sakuma had heard of Makabe's enormous size and great physical strength. Growing into a strong and powerful lad himself, Sakuma's size rivaled that of his hero and role model, and, so too, did he try to develop his own skills in the image of the great Makabe Chaan. Because of Sakuma's long arms and legs, and light but powerful body, he, like Makabe, was able to develop great leaping skills.

LAW AND ORDER IN THE CASTLE TOWN OF OLD SHURI

The Satsuma overlords maintained island tranquillity by force. This was accomplished by ensuring that local territorial administrators adhered to severe routine policies. Moreover, the Satsuma rearranged the class system in an effort to control the family lineages of the *kemochi,* and established an official department to record such information. However, together with the cumulative effects of feudalism, their efforts proved ineffective. It was during this time that King Shoko composed his satirical poem.

Poem:
> *Kamishimuya tsumete nakaya kuratatete*
> *ubaitoru uchiyu usamigurisha*
> *Shoko-O* (King Shoko, 1787–1833)

Translation:
> How poor and frugal both the upper and lower classes are now, in spite of a flourishing middle class. Ruling, during these unstable times, is so difficult.

Interpretation:
Kamishimuya refers to both the upper- and lower-classes of Okinawan people, while *nakaya* refers to the middle class. Composed by King Shoko, the poem aptly describes the dwindling condition of the kingdom, and his melancholy.

Responsible for the economic supervision of his own estate, Makabe Chaan was very familiar with the actual financial management of the upper class. It is said that because of Makabe's shrewd business talent his family was able to survive and prosper, in spite of the government's unstable financial circumstances. Yet, in the midst of a dwindling economy, Makabe Chaan was still known as the most outstanding *bushi* of his time. It is even said that the Satsuma bureaucrats recognized Makabe Chaan as Okinawa's foremost *bushi.*

Although the old castle town of Shuri seemed to be a relatively peaceful place in which to travel, Satsuma magistrates often had stones hurled at them, and were sometimes attacked in the dark of night. Every time an incident of this nature occurred, the finger of blame was pointed towards men like Makabe. For even though he may not have been the actual culprit, Satsuma officials suspected that anyone brave enough to attempt such a thing must have been trained by someone like Makabe.

In spite of his innocence, Makabe was discouraged and told his family: "The purpose of *bujutsu* is not to compete with other people, but for training all aspects of oneself. I regret having competed with so many people in the past just to prove a point. As a man sows, so shall he also reap." It is said that from that time forth, Makabe never took on another student.

According to his official resume, when Makabe was between forty and fifty years old he journeyed once to Fuzhou, China, and twice to Edo (the old name for Tokyo), on behalf of the Ministry of Foreign Affairs. It was expected that men like Makabe Chaan, "the scholar/warrior/diplomat," would one day become powerful leaders for the Ryukyu government. However, Makabe Chaan passed away during the reign of Shoko-O, at the relatively young age of fifty-five years.

Shoko-O, the nineteenth century reclusive composer king, is perhaps better remembered for the artistic masterpieces he left behind than for his political ambivalence. Because of his reclusive preoccupation with music and poetry within the walls of the royal sanctuary, Shoko-O later became known as "Boochi-usuu," the monk king.

Foreign ships appeared with increasing frequency in Okinawan waters during the reign of Shoko-O. Such sights indicated the beginning of the end of the Ryukyu Kingdom. The poem written by Shoko-O appears to reflect his anxiety over the turbulent changing social conditions of his time.

Since olden times in the Ryukyu Kingdom, Okinawans have adhered to the spiritual ritual of washing the bones of departed family members and airing out the *O-hakka* (family tomb) three and seven years after a death. In the case of Makabe Choken, we know that the date, October, 1829, indicating one of the dates his bones were washed, is inscribed on the vessel which contains his remains. Since the washing of bones is a custom performed three and seven years after one's death, one might safely conclude that Makabe died in either 1823 or 1827. Living until the age of fifty-five, it is further reasoned that he was born in either 1769 or 1773. If these calculations are correct, then it would seem that Makabe lived about two centuries ago.

In 1772, during the ongoing Satsuma oppression, an enormous *tsunami* (tidal wave) hit Miyako and Yaeyama in the Ryukyu Archipelago, taking the lives of many people. Yet, in spite of this terrifying act of God, and the taxing circumstances under the iron hand of the Satsuma, the soul of the Ryukyu people never diminished.

It was during this period of great social adversity that the spirit of the Ryukyu *bushi,* now referred to as "karate spirit," was profoundly embraced, further cultivated, and vigorously perpetuated. Surfacing as the most celebrated *bushi* of that burdensome era was *"Tobitori"* (the flying bird) Makabe Chaan, the first hero in the annals of Okinawan karate-do.

Chapter 2

To-Te Sakugawa Kanga:
The General of Great Learning,
Wisdom, and Courage

TRAVEL TO CHINA, DETENTION IN BEIJING

To-te Sakugawa's birth name was Teruya Chikudon Peichin Kanga. He was born in Shuri in 1782. After examining the old island records of Yaeyama's judicial office, Nagamine Shoshu, a Ryukyu historian living in Shuri's Kanagusuku district, imparted the following information to me. When Kanga was fifty-four years old, he became an official in Yaeyama by the order of the Ryukyu Kingdom, and was given the name of Sakugawa because of his great achievements. According to the family lineage survey carried out by Sakugawa Kantei, a descendant of the great master, To-te Sakugawa was a ninth-generation descendant of Urazoe Uekata Kuan'an, and came from the Eki Clan.

To-te Sakugawa.

Alternative suppositions suggest that Sakugawa was first sent to Yaeyama while still in his thirties to became the chief registrar of the island. This theory maintains that because of his accomplishments in Yaeyama, he received the name "Sakugawa of Nakagusuku District." If this were true, then it would seem that Teruya changed his family name to Sakugawa in his thirties rather than in his fifties. However, I feel more secure supporting the evidence from the official records of Yaeyama, than trusting folklore.

Sakugawa Kantei's information also revealed that Kanga was born across the lane from Kougibo Sokuhoku's home, the residence which once faced Osumiza Street, in Shuri, between Torihori and Akata. However, all that remains of that district these days is an empty space used as a parking lot.

The birthplace of To-te Sakugawa.

Shortly before the Americans returned control of Okinawa to Japan, I heard about an old man from Shuri's Ishimine district by the name of Sakugawa who knew many stories about To-te Sakugawa. One day, together with my student, Shinjo Kiyoshi, I visited Sakugawa's house.

Old man Sakugawa described To-te Sakugawa as an exceptionally strong and remarkably talented *bujin* who had trained since childhood. He also said that Sakugawa was intelligent and, much like Makabe Choken, had been expected since youth to advance as an important statesman for the Ryukyu Kingdom. However, it wasn't until he was in his thirties that the Ryukyu Kingdom sent Sakugawa to China as a *ryugakusei* to enhance his physical and intellectual properties.

Having a basic understanding of Okinawa's changing social matrix can improve a reader's ability to evaluate the pressure of the Satsuma during the lifetime of To-te Sakugawa. In 1844, the French Warship, *Alcmene,* arrived in Okinawa, bringing a Catholic missionary named Forcade. Its appearance indicated that the Kingdom was beginning to yield to the demands of the outside world in spite of strict Satsuma control. To protect their interests and further restrict direct commerce with the foreign presence, the Satsuma overlords confiscated local currency and issued a new Okinawan legal tender. Called Ryukyu Tsuho, all islanders were, by law, obliged to use the new currency.

The following is based on what Sakugawa from Ishimine District told me. As the book *Okinawa, 1000 Year History* describes, all tribute ships that sailed the treacherous waters between China and the Ryukyu Archipelago during feudal times were equipped with a turret, artillery, and weapons such as arrows, spears, guns, and explosives. Fast and well protected ships were necessary if the habitual attacks by coastal pirates were to be avoided or quelled. The average length of these ships was fifteen *tan* (159 meters) and they sailed in three vessel convoys. The vessels were constructed of pine and cryptomeria, or evergreen oak. Sails were woven from the leaves of "sweet flags," which are particularly resistant to wind and rain. There was a record which indicated that in 1626, King Shotei ordered ship carpenters to reinforce the hulls of all ships with this material to protect them against termites and rough seas.

It was the responsibility of the captain and crew to be able to defend their cargo and vessel against attacks during a voyage. Hence, proper training in combative disciplines was essential. Designated the official vessels of the Ryukyu Kingdom, tribute ships carried both valuable cargo and important passengers to China. Tribute was the single most important aspect of the Ryukyus' social economy, and, therefore, no expense was ever spared when it came to ensuring the safety of cargo, passengers, and crew.

The *shinkoosen* (tribute ship).

In the event of an assault, which was quite frequent during feudal times, passengers who were skilled in combative disciplines were, by order of the King, commanded to aid the crew. An example is found in the time when Sakugawa Kanga was on board such a ship bound for China. Of course, a man of Sakugawa's skills was not only expected to help, but also, in spite of being unfamiliar with ship duty, serve as an assistant to the director of security.

One evening, the day before the tribute ship was scheduled to arrive in Fuzhou, both passengers and crew were enjoying a routine voyage when, all of a sudden, the ship was attacked. Savage cries shot out from the darkness and arrows found their marks. Besieged by Chinese pirates, the crew fought gallantly against the ruthless sea dogs. A master fighter, Kanga wasted no time stripping down to his undergarment in an effort to enhance his combative mobility. Grabbing a *roku-shaku bo* (six foot staff) he bolted out on the deck of the ship under siege.

Without hesitation, Kanga moved like a whirlwind as he engaged the warrior pirates. Howling some rather browbeating lyrics in the faces of his enemy, Kanga dispatched one after another under the force of his *roku-shaku bo*. His intensity was magnified each time his weapon found its mark. Near the end of the confrontation there was one pirate who, in spite of being outnumbered, continued to avoid defeat. Just as Sakugawa was about to engage him, four or five more pirates pounced on him from behind. Unable to effectively protect himself, and in danger of being killed, Sakugawa managed to throw the attackers overboard into the dark of night, hence bringing the incident to an end. In the process, however, Sakugawa also fell into the sea. With this, Sakugawa penned the following song:

Lyrics:
> *Uchinawakamun no sukujikara shirani Bo no sachini nuchai umini nagira.*

Interpretation:
> Don't you know the reputation of Okinawa's young martial artists? We'll hurl you into the sea after first thrusting you with the end our cudgel.

Missing, and presumed dead, the chain of events following Kanga's disappearance from the tribute ship remain somewhat vague. Apparently, a Fukian naval patrol vessel on maneuvers picked up the men adrift in coastal waters the following day. Not having any reason to believe that they weren't all pirates, the Chinese ship arrested and detained them. Transported to Fuzhou, Kanga, for reasons which are not perfectly clear, was charged with piracy, not permitted to explain himself, and taken to Beijing for sentencing along with the others. By order of the Qing Magistrate, a guilty verdict brought the death penalty for the prisoners. Piracy in those times had escalated into a national problem and those found guilty as charged were executed in an effort to further deter the assaults on Ryukyu tribute ships.

In those days, condemned criminals on death row were entitled to a final meal before execution was carried out. While the pirates slopped up their food like pigs, Kanga, who had not eaten in days, protested his incarceration, and refused to touch his last meal. Chinese officials wondered about him and reported his unusual behavior to their immediate superiors. Finally, Kanga was given the opportunity to explain himself, and at long last proved his innocence. Moreover, Beijing dignitaries exalted his bravery against the pirates and rewarded him with special privileges. Such consideration permitted Kanga to remain in Beijing, where he learned Chinese boxing while pursuing his studies as a *ryugakusei,* before returning to Okinawa.

THE PROGENITOR OF SHURI-TE

Most Okinawans who wanted to learn Chinese boxing travelled to Fuzhou to study. The Chinese boxing which was brought back from

Fuzhou became especially well-known in and around Naha. Yet, when compared to the hand techniques, breathing methods, footwork, and names of the *kata* (formal exercises) of that style which was cultivated in and around the old castle district of Shuri, we observe noticeable differences. It was sometime before World War II that I first became convinced that Shuri-te also evolved from the Chinese boxing native to Fukian province. Evaluating the plausibility of this hypothesis, consider the principles of Chinese boxing being haphazardly introduced to one limited area, subjected to socio-cultural circumstances unlike that of a another time and place, and cultivated by men of different insights, physical characteristics, and attitudes. Under such varying conditions, it is entirely possible that the two traditions, in spite of having the same root origin, would develop in different ways. Hence, I believe this hypothesis provides a plausible explanation to those differences which separate karate-do in Shuri from that of Naha.

I think it would be safe to say that whatever To-te Sakugawa learned in Beijing, it unquestionably enhanced that which he had originally studied in Okinawa. Every generation produces *bujin* who, in an effort to keep discipline a living experience for the society it serves, reinterpret the common principles on which it rests. Sakugawa was one such man, a *bujin* who, by revising old village *meikata*[1] established a foundation on which a new tradition was established by the succeeding generation of students. Since Sakugawa's time, subsequent *bujin,* and varying cultural forces have influenced the growth and direction of those martial arts cultivated in and around the district of Shuri.

Continuing to study the history of Sakugawa, I came across more testimony which provided a deeper understanding of this historical figure. Oral tradition maintains that To-te Sakugawa was born in 1782, which would place his birth more than 200 years ago. Sakugawa Kangi, the father of Kantei, and a former Shuri city council member who once governed his own constituency, was able to provide me with some valuable historical material about the life of To-te Sakugawa.

Kangi confirmed that To-te Sakugawa was indeed a scholar who studied diligently in China. He also believed that he was a teacher of *kokugaku* (ancient Japanese language, thought, and culture). It is said that Sakugawa lived beyond eighty years, which would, based on Kangi's information, place his death somewhere around 1862, during the reign of Shotai-O.

Comparing oral tradition with the testimony of Kangi, and the old man from Shuri's Ishimine District, it would appear that they are similar. Killed in the Philippines during the Second World War, Sakugawa Kangi was the fifth-generation descendent of To-te Sakugawa. He was survived by his younger sister, Sakugawa Sada

The family altar of Sakugawa.

(born 1914), who (at the time of this writing) resided in Shuri.

Like many Okinawans, Sada is a spiritual person who keeps the family tablets from the Buddhist mausoleum in her home. I visited her at her home on September 1, 1985 to study the commentary of the back of the tablet of To-te Sakugawa, and was permitted to take a photograph. At that time I learned that the original tablets were, like so many other valuable objects, destroyed during the war, and that those were replicas. The only information which appeared on the new tablets was secular names.

Unfortunately, there is not much historical documentation about the *bujin* of Sakugawa's era, or Okinawa's Kingdom period in general. However, two centuries later, To-te Sakugawa is still regarded as the principal figure in the history of that fighting tradition which surfaced in Shuri. Knowing this, I knelt humbly before his memorial tablet in the house of the Sakugawa family, joined my palms together, and, in the privacy of my own thoughts, honored the memory of this great warrior.

Chapter 3

BUSHI MATSUMURA SOKON OKINA: SHURI'S BUJIN

A MASTER OF JIGEN-RYU KENJUTSU

Bushi Matsumura Sokon was born in 1809 in Shuri's Yamakawa village. Known to the Chinese as Wu Chengda, he wrote under the pen names of Unyuu and Bucho. Who first taught Matsumura *te* remains the subject of some curiosity. However, it is certain that he was interested in martial arts since childhood. From a good family, by the age of seventeen or eighteen years Matsumura had already displayed the characteristics of a promising *bujin*. Strong, intelligent, and courteous,

Portrait of Bushi Matsumura.

Matsumura learned from an early age the importance of *bun bu ryo dō* (balancing physical training with metaphysical study). In addition to his relentless pursuit of the combative disciplines, he deeply embraced Confucianism, and also became known as a brilliant calligrapher.

Having gained such a prominent reputation, Matsumura Sokon had no problem securing an occupation befitting his skills. With proper recommendations, by the age of thirty Matsumura had secured a position in the great palace of Shuri. He remained employed there until his death, serving no less than three kings: Shoko, Shoiku, and Shotai.

Bushi Matsumura was twice sent to Fuzhou and Satsuma as an envoy of the Ryukyu Kingdom. He made his last journey to Fuzhou in 1860 when he was fifty-one years old. Not only was Matsumura physically talented, he was also a man of honor respected in both Okinawa and Fuzhou. During Matsumura's generation, unlike today, great emphasis was placed on balancing physical and mental learning. Fuzhou was regarded as "the place" where such things were correctly learned. It was considered quite an achievement for a foreigner to be recognized in Fuzhou.

During Matsumura's generation, the practice of the combative disciplines, in both Fuzhou and Okinawa, took place under an iron-clad ritual of secrecy. It wasn't as if people were unaware of what was going on. Rather, the location in which martial traditions were imparted has customarily been associated with an austere sanctuary of sorts. However, an exception to the martial arts "closed-door" policy of Fuzhou was always made for a man like Matsumura Sokon. He was a man of dignity, and a man who vigorously explored the value of different schools of Chinese boxing. In addition to learning *te* in Okinawa, and *chuan fa* (*kempo*) in Fuzhou, Matsumura Sokon also mastered the principles of *Jigen-ryu kenjutsu* while stationed in Satsuma (the old name for Kagoshima in Kyushu).

I remember that it was around August of 1942 when I was researching Matsumura's family lineage that I came across a fifth-generation descendent in the Sogenji district of Naha. There, in an area nicknamed Shimaguaa, I had an opportunity to observe a rusty old Kannon (the Buddhist goddess of mercy) statue about fifteen centimeters in length, a *Jigen-ryu makimono,* and a *shikishi* (inscription card), which had been handed down in the Matsumura family. The *makimono* was so badly rotted that most of its message was unintelligible. However, I still remember one phrase clearly. It read: "When holding a sword one should be in the same mood as holding a fishing pole."

The *shikishi,* obviously written by a scholarly brush, read: *"Matsumura Peichin dono, Omokageo Miruni Nagorino Masurunari, Kimiwa kikokuo nasuto omoeba Ishuin Yashichiro"* (To Matsumura Peichin, I am extremely saddened knowing that you will soon depart, [signed] Ishuin Yashichiro). It is obvious that Ishuin was saddened by his friend's return to Okinawa. Like my other research, I too had copied this valuable document but, like all my other belongings, it was destroyed in the holocaust of October 10, 1944.

As mentioned earlier, it may serve the reader to know that the entire populated areas of greater Naha, including Shuri and Tomari, were completely annihilated by the horrifying air and naval pounding they took during the assault on Okinawa in WW II. Anything not destroyed by direct strikes, was incinerated by the perpetual fires which ensued. Countless thousands of lives were lost in the holocaust, national treasures were destroyed, ancient landmarks obliterated, important cultural property vaporized, and records of every sort simply vanished.

The rusty old statue of Kannon was a symbol of Matsumura's spiritual conviction and had been handed down in his family for five generations. There was an interesting story about Matsumura and this icon which has outlasted them both. On his return voyage to Ryukyu from Fuzhou, the ship, as was often the case sailing the waters of the East China Sea, encountered a fierce typhoon. The storm became so relentless that both passengers and crew got really scared. After a day and a night the unending tempest forced some to even cry out in fear for their lives. Only one man throughout the entire ordeal remained perfectly calm: Matsumura Sokon. While the frightened onlookers placed their fate in the hands of heaven, Matsumura trusted the goddess of mercy, and quietly chanted a *sutra* while holding his statue of Kannon.

The violent seas had blown the tiny vessel hundreds of miles north off its course, and, when the storm died down two days later, the ship had drifted to Satsuma. Accommodated by the Satsuma Ryukyukan (Okinawa's foreign outpost), passengers and crew were able to recuperate and recount the paralyzing experience at the hands of Mother Nature. Everyone was filled with admiration for Matsumura. None had ever witnessed, or even heard of, such tranquil composure under such perilous conditions. The mind of a real *bujin* was indeed a powerful thing, and Matsumura Sokon was venerated.

THE PEN AND THE SWORD

After the war I discovered that Kuwae Ryokei, the first son of Kuwae Ryosei, had returned to Okinawa from Taiwan. Having gone to Taiwan before the war, Kuwae Ryosei is regarded as the last prominent disciple of Matsumura Sokon. I had heard that Ryokei possessed a *makimono* (scroll) in Matsumura's original handwriting, and now that he was back in Okinawa I was anxious to examine it. Hence, I visited him at his home in Shuri's Torihori-cho in 1951. In addition to allowing me to study the scroll, Ryokei was kind enough to allow me to document my research photographically. Learning of my genuine regard for karate-do and the moral precepts on which it rests, Kuwae Ryokei encouraged me to write about Matsumura Sokon, and the principles for which he stood.

Matsumura's *makimono* is the oldest document in the annals of Okinawan karate-do. Besides its age, Matsumura's precepts are of

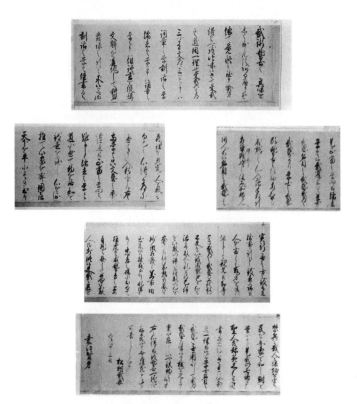

Matsumura's _makimono_

immense value. Masterfully brushed in his own hand, this document is a genuine treasure. It is believed that the scroll was written sometime after Matsumura was seventy years old. Upon scrutinizing the scroll in question, the late Okinawan master calligrapher, Jahana Unseki, was deeply impressed, and used the words "dignified" and "magnificent" to describe the strength and composure of Sokon's brush strokes. It read:

To: My Wise Young Brother Kuwae (Ryosei)

Through resolve and relentless training one will grasp the true essence of the fighting traditions. Hence, please consider my words deeply. No less interesting is the fundamental similarity between the fighting and literary traditions. By examining the literary phenomenon we discover three separate elements: 1) the study of _shisho_; 2) the study of _kunko_; and 3) the study of _jukyo_.

The study of shisho refers to commanding words and communicative skills. The study of kunko refers to a comparative study in the philosophy of ancient documents and teaching a sense of duty through example. Yet, in spite of their uniqueness, they are incapable of finding the Way. Capturing only a shallow understanding of the literary phenomenon, shisho and kunko cannot, therefore, be considered complete studies.

It is in the study of jukyo, or Confucianism, that we can find the Way. In finding the Way we can gain a deeper understanding of things, build strength from weakness and make our feelings more sincere, become virtuous and even administer our own affairs more effectively, and in doing so make our home a more peaceful place— a precept which can also apply to our country or the entire world. This then is a complete study and it is called jukyo.

Scrutinizing the fighting disciplines we also discover three divisions: 1) *gakushi no bugei*, a psychological game of strategy practiced by scholars and court officials; 2) *meimoku no bugei*, nominal styles of purely physical form, which aim only at winning (without virtue, participants are known to be argumentative, often harm others or even themselves, and occasionally bring shame to their parents, brothers, and family members); and 3) *budo no bugei*, the genuine methods which are never practiced without conviction, and through which participants cultivate a serene wisdom which knows not contention or vice. With virtue, participants foster loyalty among family, friends, and country, and a natural decorum encourages a dauntless character.

With the fierceness of a tiger and the swiftness of a bird, an indomitable calmness makes subjugating any adversary effortless. Yet, budo no bugei forbids willful violence, governs the warrior, fortifies people, fosters virtue, appeases the community, and brings about a general sense of harmony and prosperity.

These are called the "Seven Virtues of Bu," and they have been venerated by the *seijin* (sagacious person or persons; most probably Chinese Confucianists) in the document titled *Godan-sho* (an ancient journal describing the ways of China). Hence, the way of bun bu (study of philosophy and the fighting traditions, often described as "the pen and the sword") have mutual features. A scholar needs not gakushi or meimoku no bugei, only budo no bugei. This is where you will find the Way. This indomitable fortitude will profoundly affect your judgment in recognizing opportunity and reacting accordingly, as the circumstances always dictate the means.

I may appear somewhat unsympathetic, but my conviction lies strongly in the principles of budo no bugei. If you embrace my words as I have divulged to you, leaving no secrets and nothing left hiding in my mind, you will find the Way.

—Matsumura Bucho, May 13th (c.1882)

Matsumura's *makimono* is brief, but imparts an invaluable message to all those who may be unfamiliar with the true essence and aims

21

of karate-do: *bun bu ryo dō*. This emphasizes *bun bu ichi nyo,* which considers the physical and philosophical as one. There can be no question that Sokon was the man most responsible for this priceless contribution to karate-do. In fact, by way of Matsumura's *makimono,* we can conclude that he was principally responsible for proclaiming that the essence of *bu* (karate-do) in Okinawa meant cultivating these virtues, values, and principles.

If one thoroughly considers Matsumura's precepts it becomes evident that his message is the fundamental concept of humanity, and its understanding is crucial to the development of *shingitai* (lit., spirit, technique, body; referring to the development of an indomitable spirit through the use of physical technique). However, during this generation of materialism in Japan, people seem to be more preoccupied with possessions rather than the pursuit of such a spirit.

Because of this radical shift in direction, modern Japanese education has ignored the spirit of *kokoro (shin).* Too much emphasis placed on materialism has resulted in a loss of moral values. The Japanese people now face a social crisis. The time has come to learn in sincere humility the true meaning of *"karate ni sente nashi"* (there is no first attack in karate). Hence, I would like to introduce two poems which were handed down in Okinawa long ago.

Poem:
>   *Chiyuni kurusatteya ninrarishiga, chiyukuruche ninraran*

Interpretation:
>   In spite of being troubled by other people, one can still sleep.
>   However, if one troubles other people, a guilty conscience
>   makes it difficult to ever sleep soundly.

Poem:
>   *Ijinu ijiraa tei hiki, teino dejiraa iji hiki*

Interpretation:
>   Standing up for what one believes in
>   requires the balance of breath and force.
>   (too much of either is unwelcome)

These precepts were once closely associated with what has been historically described as the "Okinawan spirit." I believe that these abstracts are excellent lessons for today's *karateka.* Pondering the depth of their message one can recognize how self-control, the secret of karate-do, is the principal element in understanding that *budo* is not for fighting.

In martial arts, wherever *kokoro* has been forgotten, or never learned, so too will the principle of *karate ni sente nashi* also be misunderstood, or worse, not even known! In reality, *karate ni sente nashi* is a warning, and any martial artist who ignores this maxim is a hypocrite. There are teachers who erroneously believe that this ancient proverb simply means responding to a challenge. I say they are wrong and that responding to any challenge only condones violence. The *karate ni sente nashi* maxim is based on a poem by a famous Zen prelate named Muso Soseki (1275–1351), founder of Kyoto's Tenryu temple.

One day during a boat voyage, the priest Muso was attacked by a thug who split his head open with an oar. Caught off-guard, the *deshi* (disciple) of Muso immediately lunged to fight in retaliation. However, Muso restrained his *deshi* and chanted these words:

Poem:
> *Utsu hitomo utaruru hitomo morotomoni,*
> *tada hitohikino yumeno tawamure.*

Interpretation:
> The attacker and the defender are both nothing more
> than part of an incident in an illusion which exists
> but for only a moment in the span of one's life.

After pondering the brilliant utterance of the Zen prelate, I came to understand that rather than "not responding to the challenge," *karate ni sente nashi* really means *tatakawa zushite katsu*: victory without contention, or winning without fighting.

Another poem which compels one to consider the magnitude of *kokoro,* is the following abstract composed by a noted doctor of philosophy, Nishida Ikutaro.

Poem:
> *Waga kokoro fukaki fuchiari yorokobimo,*
> *urehino nanimo todokajito omou.*

Interpretation:
> My *kokoro* exists in an abyss so deep, it is a place which
> even the waves of joy or fear cannot disturb.

From the perspective of the martial arts, it is impossible to know the *kokoro* (spirit) of "victory without contention" if one has not yet transcended the illusion of victory or defeat: the physical boundaries of *gi* (technique) and *tai* (body).

People often concluded that the 5th-century B.C. Chinese military strategist Sun Tzu advocated the *sente* precept. Actually, we can see in his later works a proverb which more clearly illustrates his genuine intention. It suggests: "The essence of *kokoro* must surface from attraction rather than promotion if it is ever to be clearly understood. Only at that time will one's *kokoro* allow enough pliability to yield in the winds of adversity; the circumstances dictate the means. This is, so to speak, the secret of victory without contention, and it must be acknowledged." I will directly address the *karate ni sente nashi* maxim later in this book, but I would like to first return to Bushi Matsumura's story.

During his later years, Matsumura Sokon taught karate to many students at the *ochayagoten* (tea garden) in Shuri's Sakiyama district. The ochayagoten (pronounced *uchayaudon* in Okinawan) was also known as *tooen,* or east garden. During the Ryukyu Kingdom, Okinawan families of position learned *chado* (tea ceremony), *kyudo* (Zen archery), and *budo* (martial ways) in this tranquil sanctuary.

Located just next to the great castle of Shuri, the ochayagoten was often used by the royal *(Sho)* family. Unfortunately, it too was destroyed during the war. All that now remains of the ochayagoten is an empty field. However, the memories of Matsumura and those students who learned martial arts from him in that garden sanctuary live on.

The principal students of Bushi Matsumura Sokon who regularly learned from him at the ochayagoten were: Itosu Anko (1832–1916), Kuwae Ryosei (1858–1939), Yabu Kentsu (1866–1937), Funakoshi Gichin (1868–1957), Hanashiro Chomo (1869–1945), Kyan Chotoku (1870–1945), Azato Chikudon Peichin (1827–1906), Kiyuna Chikudon Peichin (1845–1920), and Sakiyama Chikudon Peichin (1833–1918).

YIELDING TO THE WINDS OF ADVERSITY

I would now like to introduce you to a rather unusual, but nonetheless stirring episode in the life of Bushi Matsumura. After king Shoko-O retired, he was called Boji-Ushu and lived in comfort at his villa in Kowan (present day Urazoe). There was a wild bull kept by a family in his neighborhood which, on occasion, would break free and trample the valuable crops in the village field. When such a thing happened people often got injured before the beast could be recaptured. This caused a lot of trouble and the villagers were very anxious about the situation. However, after Boji learned of the problem he secretly devised a plan to deal with the menace. Believing that Matsumura was a great *bujin* who could easily defeat the beast, Boji commanded that he be pitted against the bull. Considered a competent ruler, the retired king knew little about such trivial matters, and actually placed Matsumura in considerable danger by ordering such a contest.

When Shuri officials got wind of the outlandish proposal they were embarrassed. However, in spite of how ridiculous the request was, Matsumura showed no concern and simply said "How can I refuse the former king?" His only request was that he might be permitted a few days to prepare for the contest. Boji agreed and remarked, "Take as much time as you like, as long as I can see you fight the bull firsthand."

On the day of the gladiatorial-style match, people from all over packed the neighborhood. When the moment came to face the ferocious beast, Matsumura entered the arena and calmly advanced towards the bull clutching only a short wooden club in his hand. Irritated by the crowd, the bull bucked violently, snorted, and scratched the ground as it prepared to engage its adversary. When the bull charged out into the center of the arena and faced Matsumura, much to everyone's astonishment, it let out a fervent cry and ran off.

Dumbfounded, everyone including the king stood holding their breath in disbelief, until finally the king shouted: "Well done, Matsumura. You are indeed the most remarkable *bushi* in all of the world!" What the king, and the townspeople did not know was the reason why, on seeing Matsumura, the bull ran away. During the time that Matsumura was supposed to be preparing for the bout, he was actually conditioning the bull.

Under the cover of darkness, Matsumura secretly went to the animal's pen where, every night for a week, with a *konbo* (small wooden club) and dressed in the same outfit, he screamed and vigorously beat the head of the bull until even the sight or sound of Matsumura caused the beast to shudder in fear. Naturally, in the arena, when the beast got close enough to smell, hear, and see that it was Matsumura with the *konbo,* it ran off.

Following that remarkable incident the young subordinate became known throughout the kingdom as "Bushi" Matsumura, the fearless warrior. This episode really characterizes Matsumura's exceptional personality. Unlike other powerful but reckless *bujin,* Matsumura realized that a contest of strength between man and beast was meaningless, but used his wit to prove a point. It is no wonder the fighting tradition he cultivated became so popular; with such a reputation, everyone wanted to be like Bushi Matsumura.

Despite diligently searching for Matsumura's actual dates of birth and death, I was unable to locate them. The documents I once had were so badly burned from the air raid they were of no use. However,

I was able to establish what his date of birth was by conducting the following analysis: I located Uto Kaiyo, who was a very close relative of Matsumura's. She was born May 30, 1896, and lived in Shuri. Kaiyo's mother always told her that in the same year that she was born her family all attended Matsumura's *beiju* (eighty-eighth birthday) celebration. Hence, we can be sure that Matsumura Sokon was eighty-eight years old in 1896. Based on the testimony of Uto Kaiyo, it would therefore be safe to conclude that the famous *bushi* was born in 1809.

In Okinawa one's eighty-eighth birthday is regarded as a special occasion and a specific celebration, called *yuni no iwai,* is always held in honor of the celebrant. Even to this day, the *yuni no iwai* is still a major event. After all, how many of us ever make it to the age of eighty-eight?

Although it had been many years since she last uttered it, Uto Kaiyo managed to recall the lyrics of Matsumura's *yuni no iwai* poem, which her mother had taught her in childhood.

Poem:

Rukujukasaneriba hyakunijuuno utoshi,
Ukakiboshamishori wauyaganashi

Interpretation:

Sixty on top of sixty equals one hundred and twenty,
may you eat (live) until then my beloved parent.

Addendum:

During the *yuni no iwai* celebration the guests are served sixty delicious portions of tofu which have been cut into the Chinese characters, representing the number itself. The number sixty is used as the poetic epithet of the *beiju* poem. Twice sixty equals one hundred and twenty. Hence, comes the meaning, "please eat (live) until one hundred and twenty years old."

Uto Kaiyo also spoke of Tsuru-san, Bushi Matsumura's remarkable wife. The first daughter of a wealthy merchant, whose family business was known as Yonahara Yonamine, Tsuru-san had grown up as a tomboy (in fact, her name means "crane"). With a strong body, and an equally strong personality to match, most of Tsuru's friends were boys. As such, she grew up partaking in such boy's games as Okinawan sumo wrestling and *muutou* (more popularly known as *tegumi,* which, in Chinese characters, is *kumite* written backwards). Tsuru-san was a woman who surprised and impressed many. She had on occasion defeated men in feats of power by outlifting the *chikaraishi* (old style stone barbells). Among the men who came to know this remarkable woman, Tsuru-san was known as "Yonamine no Bushi Tsuru," and her reputation ultimately became well-known in and around the castle district of Shuri.

The problem, however, with being a powerful tomboy—a woman with a reputation of being stronger than men—was that nobody wanted to marry her. In Okinawa, like in Japan, if a girl does not get married while she is young, her chances of finding a suitable husband diminish in proportion to her age. With her parents becoming increasingly worried that she'd lost all chances of getting married, they offered a handsome dowry, but still attracted no candidates.

By the time Matsumura learned of Tsuru-san, he couldn't understand why no one else had jumped at the offer. Being a man who had resolved to seek spiritual enlightenment through martial arts and poverty, he had dedicated his life to king and country. To him, Tsuru-san was the ideal woman, and without delay he proposed marriage to her through her parents, as was the custom in those days.

A close and respected advisor to three Ryukyuan kings, Matsumura was a man who had successfully reinterpreted the indigenous combative methods by applying the principles of *chuan fa* and *Jigen-ryu kenjutsu*. Finding spiritual direction through Confucianism, his dedication and mastery of *budo* left a deep impression on the community from which he came. From his time forward [until the proliferation of sport karate and its commercial exploitation], the study of *To-te jutsu* (karate-do) placed great emphasis on balancing physical development with moral education. That is what is meant by the saying, *"shingitai ichinyo"* (spirit and technique are one).

Bushi Matsumura is, therefore, regarded as one of the most important historical figures in the annals of karate-do. Although the first half of his life was rather preoccupied with official undertakings in the name of king and country, the later part was not. In 1879, after the king had abdicated, his kingdom had been abolished, and Okinawa fell under the jurisdiction of prefectural control, Bushi Matsumura Sokon became reclusive and spent the remainder of his life dedicated to developing and teaching karate-do.

Even though the great Bushi Matsumura is now gone, his contributions will live on forever. I hope knowing more about the life of this great *bujin* will serve to help each of you in your own training. Matsumura's "Seven Virtues of *Bu*" will always continue to provide an important message to those who seek to understand the true meaning of *budo* through the daily practice of karate-do.

Chapter 4

MATSUMORA KOSAKU OKINA:
THE BUJIN WHO
EMPHASIZED MORALITY

KNOCKING DOWN A STALWART WITH ONLY A WET TOWEL

Matsumora Chikudon Peichin Kosaku (1829–98), was a prominent *bushi* from Tomari village, and was the first son of Matsumora Koten from the original Yuji clan, an indirect descendent of the first Sho king. Matsumora Kosaku was born on Tomari's west side, next to what is now the school in Zukeyama district, and had two brothers and four sisters. During his childhood he was called Tarukane, but was known in Chinese as Yuikan. As he grew

Portrait of Matsumora Kosaku.

into manhood, Matsumora remained rather short in height, but his wide shoulders and massive chest revealed a muscular body.

In spite of being the official port of the castle district during the Ryukyu Kingdom, Tomari village had its own administrative jurisdiction separate from Shuri. Yet the history and cultural traditions in and around this port village were not much different from that of Shuri. Although its social environment remained rather conservative, it was well known as a district from which arose a great many scholars, artists, musicians, and *bujin.*

As a boy, Tarukane studied Chinese classics and Confucianism at the school in Tomari village for young men from families of position.

28

Naturally, his education entailed learning both the social etiquette and combative skills of a *bushi*. Hence, Tarukane, like other young men of his status in Tomari, was schooled in a traditional fashion.

Since childhood, his karate teachers were Uku Giko (1800–1850) and Teruya Kishin (1804–1864), under whom he studied diligently. He was first schooled under the tutelage of Uku in the master's courtyard for three years. There, the emphasis was placed on developing a strong foundation while learning to use his legs for mobility and hips to generate power. To cultivate these fundamental skills, Master Uku taught him the three *kata* known in Tomari as Naihanchi. When it was time to begin training under the watchful eye of Master Teruya, Tarukane spent more than three years being grounded in Passai and Wanshu, the favorite *kata* of his teacher. Mastering the principal elements of his teachers' disciplines, Tarukane emerged as a powerful young *bushi*.

During that era, the practice of martial arts was never conducted in the open or beyond the confines of the courtyard. As mentioned elsewhere in this text, the fighting traditions were only taught in privacy and always cloaked in an iron-clad ritual of secrecy. There were no training facilities or public teachers available like there are today. A teacher and his student practiced secretly late at night or at dawn, usually at one's residence or in the forest near the village. However, worthy disciples who swore special oaths sometimes received the privilege of practicing at the grave site of the master.

Typical scenery of 150 years ago in and around the district of Naha. *Photo courtesy Hokama Seisho.*

Master Teruya came to admire Matsumora's enthusiasm, diligence, and remarkable talent, so much so that he ultimately invited him to continue his training at the family tomb. There, Master Teruya revealed the *bunkai* (application training) to Kosaku so that he could understand how the *kata* was used in practical ways. The family tomb was located near the Ameku Seige, far from the prying eyes of Tomari villagers.

A descendant of Bushi Matsumora Kosaku, Matsumora Kousho, deciphered the history of the Teruya family tomb for me in February of 1973. Completed in January of 1774 (according to the lunar calendar), the tomb measured 144 *tsubo* (475.2 m) and it took 122 stone-cutters forty-eight days to complete its construction at a cost of $300,000.00 (U.S.) by today's standard. Okinawan people deeply revere their ancestors and, when visiting the grave site, religiously fold their hands in prayer, as if the spirit of their ancestors were still in the tomb. Without sparing cost, they spend enormous amounts of money to build family tombs.

In the eyes of an Okinawan, nothing was as important as the character or personality of a potential *deshi* (disciple) of karate. There was, and to some extent still is, an unwritten law that karate should never be taught to anyone who is rude, arrogant, or disrespectful, and that

also held true for brothers and children of the master's family. The reason Master Teruya taught Matsumora at the family tomb was not only because he was so talented, but largely because he was a modest and genuine person; a man who understood that the essence of karate was *shingitai* and deeply embraced its principles. To Master Teruya, Matsumora was the perfect *deshi*. Hence, it was at the family tomb in front of Teruya's ancestors,

Author pays respects to the Teruya family tomb where Kosaku made his pledge and trained secretly.

that master and *deshi* sincerely exchanged vows. For Matsumora, this honor reinforced his commitment, well being, and enthusiasm to continue his training even harder than ever before.

There was a cave, nicknamed Furuherin, about 200 meters away from the family tomb, which a recluse used as his sanctuary. Living there, he soon became aware of the daily exchange between master and disciple, and often secretly observed their training. One day while Matsumora was practicing his *kata* by himself, he let go a kick with a sharp *kiai*. As he turned for the next move he unexpectedly made eye contact with the recluse, who, acknowledging Matsumora's presence, just turned and nonchalantly stepped back into the cave. During an era when the practice of martial arts was so secret, Matsumora was surprised by the man's lack of curiosity. Matsumora's intuition told him that there was something special about this recluse. Notwithstanding, he concluded his training and returned home early that day. Matsumora was unable to fall asleep quickly that night in anticipation of his early morning training. Impatient for dawn to come, he ran to his teacher's house to tell him about the old man in the cave. Master Teruya responded by saying "He sounds quite mysterious, you should go and pay a visit to him by yourself."

That evening Matsumora politely visited the old man at the cave and was welcomed with a smile. The recluse apologized to Matsumora for disturbing his private training and also commended the level of his skill. Taking out an old piece of paper from his garment, the recluse handed it to Matsumora, and left the cave quietly. On the paper was inscribed the following: *"Bu wa shinjitsunari. Kokoro wa kokoro o motte migaku. Shikashi gi wa taizan yori omoshi. Kore bu no shinzui nari."* After reading the paper Kosaku looked for the recluse but he was nowhere to be found in the darkness. He called out for the old man but received no reply. He even waited for him to return but to no avail. The stranger was gone. Reluctantly, Matsumora went home. Showing the paper to his master, Teruya responded by saying, "Exactly!" but never said another word.

The author visiting the cave where the recluse lived.

The mysterious recluse was never again seen or heard from. Pondering the underlying message of the abstract lesson left to him by the recluse, Matsumora was unable to analyze its value and became increasingly tormented. Then one rainy day while he was listening to Master Teruya, Matsumora had a flash of insight and in a moment understood the underlying meaning of the message left to him by the old recluse: "The essence of *bu(do)* is to denounce immoral consideration, understand humanity, follow a virtuous path, and devote your life to cultivating peace in Okinawa."

During Matsumora's era, the school in Tomari not only served as a place of learning but also as a gathering point for the men of the village. One day the young men of the village sat around in a circle in the schoolyard discussing the escalating injustice of Satsuma officials in Okinawa. As the heat of their discussion intensified, their hostility clearly became evident. The recent assaults on women and children during routine inspections by the Satsuma had provoked fear and anger among locals. "If it happened in Tomari," they said, "we would ring the emergency bell, collect our men, and protect the village by ourselves." Unable to forgive the shameless acts of rape and violence, Matsumora nodded in agreement. There could be no question that the Satsuma had no respect for any Okinawan or their liaison with the Middle Kingdom, China.

From that day forward, Matsumora reinforced the effectiveness of his style by contriving a way in which to disarm a swordsman with only the use of a wet towel. Having his *deshi* attack him with a wooden sword, Matsumora employed *taisabaki* (maneuvering the body in an effort to gain a superior position by shifting foot position), as the necessary element needed to overcome a swordsman. By wrapping stones inside the wet towel it became an effective means of breaking a sword or incapacitating an adversary. Practicing diligently for days, Matsumora was finally able to disarm his *deshi* even under rapid attacks.

One day when Matsumora was on Haariya Street, between the Takahashi Bridge and Maemichi Street in the neighborhood of Yamazato Giki, he heard screams coming from among a crowd of angry people. As he got closer he saw a Satsuma official in the midst of the crowd holding up his sword and bellowing out "What did you say? Come here you little insolent bastard, you're nothing but a bunch of low-life scum!" Witnessing such despicable behavior prompted Matsumora to respond immediately. Pushing his way through the crowd he lunged right in front of the foreign official. The crowd was astonished, as was the sword wielding samurai. For anyone to stand up to a Satsuma swordsman, with or without a sword of his own, was an unthinkable demonstration of courage.

Standing in the face of danger, Matsumora quickly removed the moist Japanese towel which he had recently been in the habit of carrying concealed inside his garment. Then, without warning, the infuriated swordsman took a mortal swipe at Matsumora. Without even as much as a blink of an eye, Matsumora's evasive action moved him outside the range of the deadly blow as the crowd scattered for safety. Flinging the towel at the astonished warrior he was able to wrap it around his sword and yank it from his grip. However, in the struggle Matsumora lost his little finger as the sword flew to the ground. As quickly as he had flung the towel, Matsumora lunged out and recovered both the sword and his severed finger, hurling them both into the Azato River before dashing away. With a complete loss of face, the overcome samurai swiftly withdrew. Losing one's sword in battle was, for any samurai, a loss of spirit. However, for a samurai of the fierce Satsuma *han*, to lose his sword to an Okinawan was an unimaginable disgrace.

In complete awe, the entire neighborhood witnessed the unbelievable confrontation from behind the safety of the nearby bushes and stone wall. The brave *bushi* from Tomari had not only rescued them from danger, he had also removed any fear of Satsuma retaliation by publicly humiliating the foreign official. After the brief but intense encounter, everyone quietly dispersed in twos and threes, remembering that which had just occurred in the neighborhood of Yamazato Giki.

Only about twenty years old, and having lost his finger in the encounter, Matsumora was deeply concerned about the safety of the other villagers. There could be no question that if officials came looking for him he would not be too difficult to locate with a freshly severed finger. Hence, that night he secretly departed from Tomari to hide out in Nago's Asoubaru district. As Matsumora had expected, government officials from the Satsuma bureau came to the school a couple of days later looking for him. However, Tomari townspeople wore an air of innocence throughout the entire ordeal, maintaining that there were no young men in their village who'd recently lost a finger. Unable to find their man, the detachment left without satisfaction. The Tomari villagers never saw or heard from them again.

With the Ryukyu Archipelago's escalating economic instability, Nago's Asoubaru district continued to be a place were many *bushi* from Shuri, Naha, and Tomari congregated after losing both their stipend and position. After settling down, and with the help of a friend, Matsumora was able to secure a position as a rent collector with the largest landowner in that area. As was often the case, the tenant farmers often fell behind in their payments, in spite of their honest intentions. However, thanks to Matsumora's character and reputation the tenant/landowner relationship improved as did the farmers' ability to pay their rent. This brought favorable attention to Matsumora from the landowner and resulted in him becoming a popular figure in the village. During his free time Matsumora taught the young villagers Chinese classics, calligraphy, and martial arts. In spite of the young men not showing much interest in martial arts, Matsumora never for a moment forgot his responsibility to training. During his period of self-exile in Nago, Matsumora decided that when the time was right he would return to Tomari and continue his pursuit along the path of the martial arts.

While residing in Nago, Matsumora lived in a forest area called Hichiya Mui, far away from any other villagers. His abode was about two kilometers from Mayaga, which is presently the Asahikawa district. Having access to a large property, Matsumora was able to scatter various apparatuses for training here and there. Among the various training instruments he used were the *chikaraishi* (stone barbells and dumbbells) and *makiwara* (striking posts). With the land presently being used as a sweet potato farm, it is difficult to imagine it as the onetime training area for Bushi Matsumora.

At any rate, Matsumora continued to train himself relentlessly and did his best to remember and adhere to the precious words left to him by the old recluse at Furuherin cave. In spite of living in the forest, Matsumoa needed only to close his eyes to see Shuri in the privacy of his own mind. During these times, he prayed for the peace and security of his country, and his master. When he became overcome by loneliness, Matsumora sometimes plucked his *shamisen* and sang Ryukyu folk tunes. The following was one of his favorites.

Poem:
> *Yuinmo akachikenmo narishi umukajino tatanu*
> *hiyanesami suyano chimuri.*

Interpretation:
> Like the never ending smolder of boiling salt from seawater
> on the beach, the memory of your image permeates
> my soul from the crack of dawn until the dusk of day.

BECOMING AN EXPERT IN BOJUTSU IN SPITE OF LOSING A FINGER

To Matsumora, the succeeding ten years or so had passed quickly as a dream. Hearing that the situation in Tomari village had changed for the better, Matsumora decided to return to his hometown. Returning to Tomari without incident, he took up residence on the west side of the elementary school across from Yuhinaguwa, in the district of Ie. At the time of his return, weaving had become a popular business in Tomari village. Fortunately, during his stay in Nago, Matsumora had established a bond of friendship with a family from Yamanuhabaru's Izumi district who were producers of indigo, an important ingredient in weaving. Matsumora was able to earn a decent living trading with the weavers and the indigo producers.

In the succeeding years, while in Yanbaru on business, Matsumora got the opportunity to study *Jigen-ryu jojutsu* directly under the tutelage of Chatan Yara (Master Yara from Chatan village). Then the superintendent in charge of the King's riding stable in Makibaru, Yara was regarded as a master of several combative traditions. Learning under this taskmaster, Matsumora deepened his understanding of the fighting traditions in general.

Back in Tomari village, the town seniors still often gathered at the old school to enjoy the company of friendly conversation. After all the years which had passed, the old village school was still a popular spot for locals to meet and discuss martial arts. One day, as was often the case, the seniors were gathered around discussing a man named Toguchi from Kaneku. "Recently this young man has gained quite a reputation for himself," one of the seniors remarked. "In spite of having a physical handicap, he has overcome his impediment and his skill with a *bo* (wooden staff) is regarded as outstanding," the old man continued to say. "He is able to do some remarkable things with his *bo*. For example, recently he was seen to have made a hole in a large ceramic container with only a short thrust of his *roku-shaku bo,* and on another occasion he picked up and heaved an 18kg sack with the same *bo.*"

The senior concluded by saying that Toguchi-san's skills were equalled only by his modest character. In that conversation Toguchi was also compared to Matsumora, who, although no longer in his prime, was still regarded as incomparable. Knowing that Matsumora had since enhanced his *bojutsu* with the principles of *jojutsu,* the group wondered who might prevail in a contest between the two. The idea warranted action; hence, the two men were petitioned by the seniors. In those days, whether one liked it or not, nobody could refuse the order of seniors. With the bout set to be held in the open space near the gate beside the village school, the contestants prepared to meet each other.

Matsumora had strengthened his combative abilities by mastering the secret *jojutsu* technique of *Jigen-ryu* taught to him by Chatan Yara. The length of his *Jigen-ryu jo* was four *shaku,* two *sun,* and one *bu* (approximately 1.3 meters), and the seniors were eager to observe how Matsumora used the *Jigen-ryu jo,* in spite of his missing finger. As Matsumora took grip of his weapon and entered the enclosure he remembered the words of Chatan Yara: *"Toru jo no nigiri choshi wah yawarakaku, shimezu yurumezu koyubihanasazu,"* which translates as "Without releasing the little finger, one's grip should be pliable, not stiff."

Keeping this idea in mind, Matsumora faced his younger opponent with a natural posture and a pliable grip on his *jo.* There were those watching who doubted the strength of Matsumora's *kamae* (combative posture) because it seemed to lack authority. Toguchi, on the other hand, moving with lightning speed and aiming the *bo* directly at Matsumora's throat, looked menacing. The two faced each other for a while before gradually inching their way to within engagement distance. The next step would certainly determine victory or defeat; they were so close to each other that it was suffocating.

Like two animals in the frightening moments just prior to lunging at each other in mortal combat, the two combatants faced each other prepared to do battle. Matsumora was calm, relaxed, and confident; Toguchi was young, powerful, and tense. The beads of sweat illuminating his taut forehead in the heat of the afternoon sun now made Toguchi's uncertainty obvious. That which Matsumora had already noticed moments before was now clearly evident to the seniors as well. Toguchi had lost his composure.

The longer they stood facing each other the more obvious it became that Matsumora's intense conviction overwhelmed Toguchi's fluttering ambivalence. Realizing his own inward uneasiness, Toguchi retreated from the forcefulness of Matsumora's presence. With Toguchi's back nearly to the stone wall now, everyone could tell that the end was near. Unnerved, and unable to move back any further, the sound of Toguchi's *bo* hitting the ground and his deep breathing made it clearly evident that he was no match for the more confident Matsumora Kosaku. "*Tatakawa zushite katsu* (victory without contention)," Matsumora had defeated Toguchi without as much as a single blow. Toguchi had been intimidated by the intensity of Matsumora's confidence, his unusual *kamae,* and his own self-doubt.

Yet, in spite of his defeat at the hands Matsumora, Toguchi's reputation spread throughout the village. For any man to overcome his physical handicap, master the cudgel, and then face the great Bushi Matsumora in combat, regardless of the outcome, was a personal victory far more important than the details of any encounter. The exploits of these two stalwarts gave birth to a local expression which personified the caliber of martial arts in Tomari: "In Tomari even the handicapped are *bujin.*" Bushi Matsumora Kosaku was thirty-four years old at the time.

In September of 1872, a delegation was sent to Tokyo to attend a special congratulatory celebration commemorating the establishment of the Meiji government. Led by Prince Shoken and his subordinate Giwan Choho, the group included Yamazato Choken and Kishaba Choken along with about 100 other statesmen. Receiving such VIP status pleased the Okinawan contingent very much. However, when it was announced that King Shotai, under the new Meiji government, would have to abdicate and the Ryukyu Kingdom be abolished, they were deeply humiliated. Unable to oppose the mandate, the despondent group returned home. As one could imagine, many of the Ryukyu *kemochi* (aristocracy) were very indignant over this scandalous incident. Labeled a traitor, Giwan Choho became the scapegoat of the people and was forced to resign his position as *Sanshikan* (one of the three top positions in political office).

In the decades prior to the abolition of the Kingdom, during the era when Japan had just made the transition from feudalism to democracy and the nation was being unified, there were mixed pockets of resistance in the Ryukyu Kingdom. On the one hand, loyal zealots wanted to preserve the Kingdom's hierarchy and all it represented. On the other hand, however, a growing movement envisioned a closer relationship with the Japanese. Giwan Choho was one such man. Representing active participation with the Japanese, Giwan's political faction was called the *Kaikatou,* or Open Country Party, and was often referred to as the Shiruha, or White Sect.

In opposition to the *Kaikatou* was the *Ishimakuratou,* or Stone Pillow Party, headed by former *Sanshikan* statesman Kamekawa Uekata Moritake. The *Kuruha,* or Black Sect as it was sometimes called, sought to gain independence from Japan and share friendly relations with China. Friction between the two sects continued to intensify day by day.

The principal politicians of the Stone Pillow Party in Tomari village were Kuba Choryo, Matayoshi Kaho, and Matayoshi Choho. Also a staunch supporter of this hard line party, Bushi Matsumora Kosaku was responsible for the physical training of young recruits. On behalf of the faction, Matsumora organized and trained a group of young men who would, in a moment, lay down their lives to protect the Ryukyu Kingdom. Collecting men from around Tomari village, Matsumora trained the youths in the big old vegetable garden of Higa Moko's residence on Kushimichi Street. Day and night they trained diligently in an effort to strengthen their force. Aware of their clandestine activities, the opposition tried to infiltrate the organization by sending spies to gather intelligence.

In the years that passed between 1843 and 1847, British and French warships appeared in Ryukyuan waters. Then in 1853, Commodore Perry sailed into the port of Tomari and made his forceful appearance at the great castle of Shuri. Matsumora worried deeply about both the domestic and foreign pressures that the Ryukyu Kingdom was facing. Compared to the relative tranquility of his home during the time when he hid out in the mountains of Nago, the political, economic, and social unrest of the Ryukyu Kingdom had been transformed into something unlike anything he had ever known before.

British and French warships at port in Naha. Photo from the *History of Okinawa*.

With internal turmoil of its own, even China was unable to offer any military assistance. What little political lobbying it asserted was of even less help to the tiny satellite colony. Control of the Ryukyu Kingdom had, in essence, been handed over from the Tokugawa governed Satsuma to the new Meiji government, and the Ryukyuan people had no control over their future. With such unrest, Matsumora concluded that it was up to men like himself to uphold and carry on the Ryukyu culture and justice. Hence, Bushi Matsumora Kosaku formed a coalition with Oyadomari Kokan (1827–1905) and Yamazato Gikei (1835–1905). Together, these three men were called "Tomari's Big Three."

The widespread feeling of those loyal zealots can be best remembered by the poems Oyadomari Kokan, the oldest of the three, composed.

Poem:

Uchinan ushinariba ichashiikekariga,
ushuganashi otomo ano yomaden.

Interpretation:

If our Kingdom is destroyed, how can we continue to live?
We'll die defending the king.

Poem:

Yamatunchuyakara ikachiukariyumi,
shininyamatsukute tomoniikana.

Interpretation:

How can the Japanese possibly prevail when we're
prepared to die on top of a mountain of Japanese bodies.

Finalizing their pledge to each other in what might have been their final meeting, the Big Three exchanged farewell drinks of water from ceremonial sake cups. According to the *bujin* code of conduct, Matsumora's actions were justified. Standing up for his convictions was everything Matsumora had learned from Uku, Teruya, and the old recluse at Furuherin. Diligently practicing the fighting traditions every day, and then teaching and imparting the philosophy on which it rested to the young men of his village, Bushi Matsumora had, according to martial art's protocol, repaid his obligation.

In addition to the martial arts and political facets of his life,

The *Haari* boat races.

Bushi Matsumora vigorously supported Okinawa's *Haari* boat races. A magnificent festival held in Naha's Irie district on the 4th of May every year, according to the lunar calendar, its purpose was to ensure continued peace and abundant harvest throughout the Ryukyu Kingdom. A tradition which traces its history back to the time of Satto-O (1350–1422), the festival features three brightly colored sea-going vessels competing against each other. Blue belonged to Naha and represented Yamato (the Japanese); yellow belonged to Kume and represented China; and black belonged to Tomari and represented the Ryukyu Kingdom. An important cultural event which continues even to this day, the Haari boat races are on a scale of importance with the Tug of War festival.

The magnitude of this event provoked such enormous excitement that spectators and competitors often died in the midst of the race. Hence, this problem became known as *Haarimundou*. In an effort to reduced the danger for Tomari villagers, Kosaku was made helmsman because of his powerful martial arts skills and leadership qualities. It is said that from the time that Bushi Matsumora was invited to represent Tomari, the *Haarimundou* ceased to exist. There is an old Tomari folk song I would like to introduce.

Folk song:
> *Kono ninju surute Shuriganshi medei ijitachuru tokeya*
> *sabiya nesami; kurimade gayayura matta ichegashabira*
> *kyo no ijitaiya sadamegurisha haari Tomaino hensaayo.*

Interpretation:
> In the service of the King from Shuri we are a strong force of people, and need not be lonely when we leave. Because nobody knows the boundaries of life and death, this might be our last moment to live.

PROTECTOR OF THE NEEWAGUMUCHI

The year 1879 marked the official end of the Ryukyu Kingdom and witnessed the establishment of the prefectural system under which Okinawa's political administration fell. With the establishment of this system, just about every facet of Okinawan society was radically changed. Not beyond the long reach of this power, so, too, did King Shotai have to abdicate his throne and relocate to Tokyo. During this chaos, the entire Ryukyuan population fell into great disarray.

As was the custom during the old kingdom period, each village came to possess, to greater or lesser degrees, its own collective property and savings. In Tomari, it was the slope areas located on the northeast boundary of the village known as Kuganemui and Takamasai. The collective savings, for the most part, represented an endowment from Yamazato Choken, and was called *Neewagumuchi*. A benevolent man, Yamazato Choken had donated his own annual stipend in an effort to provide a better future for the underprivileged youth of Tomari village. Although academically brilliant, young Yamazato was desperately poor.

Passing the most difficult national examination of the Ryukyu Kingdom, Yamazato was one of only three out of five hundred to make the grade. His grades permitted him to acquire an elite position

39

within the government of the old kingdom. After working hard and making further sacrifices, Yamazato saved his entire annual salary and donated it to Tomari village. Those funds became known as *Neewagumuchi* and were managed separately from the official finances of the kingdom. However, after the new system was enacted, Japanese officials tried to claim both the collective property and *Neewagumuchi* as the public property of the Meiji Government.

As a principal of the Stone Pillow Party, Matsumora Kosaku could not stand by and watch such an injustice take place. "It's time to put the philosophy of the martial arts into action rather than just depending on its physical counterpart. Loyalty is far greater than even China's Mt. Taishan," said Matsumora. Hence, Matsumora gathered together the young men whom he had trained and explained the situation to them. Emphasizing the need to combat injustice, all the young men agreed, quivering with excitement in anticipation of the forthcoming crusade.

Several days later, some important government officials appeared in Tomari to negotiate the transfer of the property and funds. Held at the Uku residence in Yuwayasuji, the village seniors sat face-to-face with the government officials asserting their claim to both the land and the capital. However, the meeting got out of hand and escalated into a heated quarrel. Frightened by the throng of young men with wooden staves *(bo)* and iron truncheons *(sai)* in their hands gathered in the courtyard of Uku's residence, the government officials refrained from reaching an agreement. Unsatisfied with the decision, Tomari's seniors protested the procrastination.

Shortly thereafter, another consultation was held between Meiji officials and Tomari village seniors. That encounter was held at the Tamanaha residence in Yuwagura. Like before, they again sat down face-to-face, but this time the *Neewagumuchi* was placed in the middle of the room in a vault box. In a malevolent tone, the seniors of Tomari village bellowed at the foreign politicians: "Go ahead, take it away if you dare." In the courtyard, like at Uku's residence, Matsumora's men were assembled, only this time they called the Meiji officials' actions inequitable and taunted them bellowing out "go ahead, try to take it if you can."

Matsumora's intimidation tactics worked. The Meiji officials reasoned that the Tomari villagers were willing to fight to the end for that which they believed was lawfully theirs. The officials left and did not confiscate the land or money. This account was documented in Tomari's official book of village records.

From that time, the *Neewagumuchi* continued to be protected by the elders of Tomari village and was handed down through the Meiji, Taisho, pre-war, and post-war eras until 1974. Then, on

August 3rd, the capital was used to establish the Senkaku Kenshokai Corporation of Tomari, an official organization founded for the welfare of Tomari village.

Supported by the Senkaku Kenshokai, a special anniversary celebration was held at the Komyo meeting hall in Tomari on February 5, 1984, to commemorate the history of the *Neewagumuchi*. The unprecedented gathering included thirty-seven people who were seventy years of age, twenty-four people who were eighty-five years of age, and one person who was ninety-seven years of age.

Thanks to the loyalty of Bushi Matsumora, the charitable endowment of Yamazato Choken has remained secure for nearly two centuries. Yamazato's great contribution and Matsumora's enormous risk represent classic examples of Tomari honor and tradition. They will forever serve to remind future generations of what loyalty, unselfishness, and true honor mean to the *Uchinanchu* (Okinawan people).

In March of 1879, when Bushi Matsumora Kosaku was fifty-one years old, King Shotai abdicated, officially bringing an end to the Ryukyu Kingdom. Although Matsumora was in the late prime of his life, his power and skills never wavered. During that time there were two promising young stalwarts from Shuri who came to Tomari to visit the famous Bushi Matsumora. They were Motobu Choyu (1865–1929), and Yabu Kentsu (1866–1937), and in spite of good intentions, their overenthusiasm colored them somewhat rude. Yet, the wise Matsumora knew that these were not mischievous young men looking to make a name for themselves, rather, they were honestly curious but hopelessly green seekers.

Knowing that the men had come for an experience, Matsumora invited them to test his strength. "Well gentlemen," said Matsumora, "I'm going to just sit down and place both of my feet flat on the edge of the porch. I want you to try to lift me up if you can." With a chuckle, the two men knew that it must be a trick, as it was far too easy a task.

Yanking on Matsumora's arms with all their might, the two were unable to move him more than an inch. Feeling a little embarrassed, both Motobu and Yabu decided to make their exit in a manner less noticeable than their appearance. Just then Matsumora told them that "one should never give up quite so easily, nor is it wise to judge someone by their age." Before the two young men from Shuri left, Matsumora also taught them the value of non-resistance in *budo* by describing the ancient proverb "Ryusui saki o kisowazu," or "Flowing water never competes with anything in its path."

Bushi Matsumora had avoided trouble since childhood. In spite of difficult times he had also, through diligence and sacrifice, remained dedicated to the virtues, values, and principles of martial arts (karate-do). Both before and after the King abdicated and the kingdom was abolished, the great Bushi of Tomari distinguished himself as a truly great *bujin*. Departing this world in November of 1898 at the age of seventy, the loyal *bushi*, Matsumora Chikudon Peichin Kosaku, is now regarded as the central figure most responsible for cultivating the fighting traditions in and around the village of Tomari.

The fighting traditions of Bushi Matsumora were handed down to Yamazato Giki (1866–1946), Kuba Koho (1870–1942), and Iha Kodatsu (1873–1928). Of these three, it was Master Iha who was most responsible for teaching karate to so many young people at the Tomari Student Association. In fact, I enjoyed the privilege of learning the Tomari *Passai, Chinto, Wankan, Rohai,* and *Wanshu kata* directly from Master Iha. Even to this day I continue to preserve and study these profound *kata* at my own school.

Learning the *kata* of Bushi Matsumura Sokon through Kyan Chotoku, and the kata of Matsumora Kosaku through Motobu Choki, I am of the third generation to preserve and pass on these invaluable traditions from their time. In an effort to preserve and pass on this valuable cultural heritage, I institutionalized these teachings in July of 1947. Commemorating the lives of both Bushi Matsumura and Bushi Matsumora, I selected the

Author Shoshin Nagamine and his son Takayoshi Nagamine practice kumite at the graveyard of the Matsumora family ancestors. 1986

first Chinese character used in each of the surnames of Matsumura and Matsumora, to establish the Matsubayashi *ryuha*. Hence, the Matsubayashi-ryu tradition not only combines the defensive legacy of both Shuri and Tomari, it also underscores the virtues, values, and principles on which this legacy rests.

I mentioned in the beginning of this chapter that Matsumora Kosaku came from the Yuji clan which originally came from the royal (Sho) family of the old Ryukyu Kingdom. In continuing my research into the life of Matsumora Kosaku I was able to locate the present day whereabouts of the Yuji family and requested the assistance of Matsumura Hajime and Matsumura Kosho, both from that genealogy.

Descendants of the Yuji clan connected to Matsumora Kosaku's family were forced to reside in several different localities during the post-war period. However, in an effort to bring family relatives back into contact with each other, the Tokiwah Association was organized. During that time, the organization encountered difficulty raising sufficient funds to erect a stone monument commemorating the life of Bushi Matsumora. Because of my strong connection with Bushi Matsumora through karate-do, I was subsequently asked to assist them in their campaign. I imme-

The Matsumora monument.

diately agreed to not only assist them in their campaign to construct the monument, but also to support the Tomari Senkaku Memorial Association as well.

On May 8, 1983, the *kenshohi* monument, commemorating the life of Bushi Matsumora, was erected in Tomari's Arayashiki park. Given the great honor of writing the epitaph on the stone monument, I would like to conclude this chapter with those final words:

Matsumora Kosaku (1829–98) was born in Tomari village. Remarkably talented, the *bushi* from Tomari was a man who took full advantage of his small but powerful body. As a youth, Matsumora studied the fighting traditions of Tomari village under Uku Giko and Teruya Kishin. Under the astute tutelage of teachers like Uku and Teruya, so too did Matsumora ultimately distinguish himself as a brave *bujin*. He became well known for his chivalry and vibrant spirit, and was well remembered for once preventing a sword-wielding Satsuma samurai from harming Tomari villagers. Then, in an effort to avoid any subsequent repercussions, he confined himself in obscurity in a remote part of Nago. Matsumora is also remembered for his efforts to protect specific village property and a special communal endowment in the name of Governor Yamazato Choken, known as the *Neewagumuchi*. By 1879, both the property and legal tender of this sizable contribution were in danger of being confiscated by the Meiji Government after the King abdicated and the kingdom was abolished. However, the efforts of Japanese officials to confiscate the special assets of Tomari village were thwarted thanks in large part to the efforts of Bushi Matsumora and his diligently trained supporters. Since Matsumora's historical efforts, the *Neewagumuchi* has been meticulously managed until it was ultimately used to establish the *Senkaku Kenshokai*, a society that continues on even to this very day. In knowing this, the name of Kensei (Fist Saint) Matsumora Kosaku, a man of honor and justice, will live on forever.

Written on this auspicious day in May, 1983, and sponsored by the Yuji Family Society: An association which established the monument to commemorate the life of Matsumora Kosaku; president Matsumura Kosho, and all other Tokiwa-kai members. Nagamine Shoshin, the President of Matsubayashi-ryu Karate-do Kodokan and his membership. The membership of the nonprofit Tomari Senkaku Kenshokai directed by Board Chairman Maeda Giken.

Chapter 5

ITOSU ANKO OKINA:
A PROMINENT MODEL OF CHIVALRY

THE MODEL OF CHIVALRY

Itosu Anko was the early master of karate whose courage prevented him from ever being drawn into a fight. Posthumously named Kensei (Fist Saint), Itosu was regarded as a model of chivalry. Commemorating the life and enormous contributions of this remarkable man, a stone monument was constructed and erected beside the great master's grave site in the forest of Furushima in Mawashi on August 30, 1964.

Portrait of Itosu Anko.

By post-war Okinawa, Chibana Choshin was the only remaining personal disciple of Itosu Anko. In an effort to commemorate the life of his great teacher, Chibana brought together relatives, family descendants, and interested people to fulfill the commemorative stone monument project. His selfless efforts, done only to repay his teacher's kindness, resulted in bringing Chibana considerable recognition in a prudent community. His efforts not only served to invigorate the karate community in Okinawa but helped restore a sense of pride and loyalty obliterated by war.

The inscription on Itosu's stone monument reads:

Itosu Anko was born in Shuri's tiny hamlet of Gibo in 1831. He died in Yamakawa village in March of 1915, at the age of eighty-five. Having mastered the principles of karate-jutsu, Itosu Anko dedicated his entire life to the development of modern karate-do. Itosu Anko is recognized as the man most responsible for bringing karate out from behind its closed doors of obscurity and introducing it into the school system, where it first served as an adjunct to physical education. His immeasurable contributions provided the very foundation on which modern karate-do was established.

The establishment of this commemorative monument marks the fiftieth anniversary of his death and the enormous achievements preserved and passed on by the students of Itosu Anko.

August 30, 1964.
Established by the Kobayashi-ryu Karate-do Kyokai
President, Chibana Choshin
Calligrapher, Iraha Choko
Engraver, Ishimine Jitsuhiko.

Traditionally, the biographies of historical *bujin* have always recounted a tale of physical confrontation and gallantry. However, in the case of

The Itosu stone monument.

Itosu Anko there is no such history. In his eighty-five years there was not a single episode describing such an encounter. Highly skilled in the fighting traditions, the very fact that Itosu avoided physical confrontation, especially during the time of his generation, is in itself testimony that he was a man of eminent virtue.

Because the Okinawans were prohibited from trading directly with foreign powers by the *bakufu* (Edo government), the appearance of British ships in the Ryukyu Kingdom around the time of Itosu's birth marked the beginning of an era of escalating political instability. Itosu was born just three years before Shoiku ascended to the throne, and was forty-eight years old when Shotai, Okinawa's last king, abdicated in 1879.

As a child, Itosu was introverted and rather small when compared to other boys his age. Some say that it was his size that made him such a quiet child, others say it was his strict home life. Whatever the case, there can be no question that Itosu was extremely shy in his youth. Brought up in the traditional settings of the *kemochi* (a family of position) the young Anko underwent a typically strict upbringing.

Educated in the Chinese classics and calligraphy, Itosu grew into a fine young man and showed a remarkable aptitude in writing skills. In fact, so good was his calligraphy and character that he later gained a position as a secretary for the *soushi koori* (administrative office) of the Ryukyu Kingdom in Shuri. According to the Ryukyu historic dictionary, *soushi koori* represented the highest level of administration during the Shuri kingdom. In short, it was responsible for overseeing each of the kingdom's most powerful land owners.

A rear view of Itosu's stone monument.

As was often the case with young men from families of position, Itosu was schooled in *to-te* (karate), the martial tradition of his day. Taking his first lesson under the watchful eye of Nagahama Chikudon Peichin, Itosu quickly matured into a powerful disciple and ultimately became the personal protege of the distinguished Bushi Matsumura. In time, Itosu became known as Bushi Matsumura's foremost disciple. A role model if ever there was one, Itosu Anko trained vigorously until his death in 1915 at the age of eighty-five, and had a profound impact on the evolution of modern karate-do.

Like many other prominent families which traced their roots back to China, so too did the Itosu family consider Confucianism a principal source of spiritual direction.[2] In the Itosu residence there was a room which served as a spiritual sanctuary, a place where daily worship and meditation could be practiced without interruption.

Of the many symbols representing the Itosu family's regard for the spiritual was an icon at the center of the family shrine which read *"keiten"* (i.e., respect Heaven). In the *tokonoma* (alcove) there hung a silk scroll with a masterfully brushed Ryukyuan poem which read: "By honoring the virtue of respect one will never lose direction, even during a generation of deteriorating values."

Their tiny Buddhist altar was always immaculately clean with fresh flowers placed on it the 1st and 15th day of every month. Every day before the family members ate their meals, a small offering of food and tea was meticulously placed on the altar as a sign of spiritual dedication. For Buddhists, this is a ritual which continues to be strictly adhered to, even to this very day. In describing the home of Grandmaster Itosu, I am reminded that is was Oshiro Chojo (1888–1939), a prominent master of *Yamanni-ryu bojutsu* who also learned karate under Itosu Sensei, who first told me about his teacher's house in Ounak-cho. From a home which placed enormous importance on traditional values came Itosu Anko, a gracious man of profound virtue.

Avoiding physical violence his entire life, Itosu trained with incredible ferocity and found contentment putting his heart and soul into his *makiwara* practice. Having studied directly under the personal guidance of Bushi Matsumura, Itosu and his *dohai* (classmate) Kiyuna Peichin were regarded as two of the master's most unique *bujin*. Well known among Matsumura's many students, both Itosu and Kiyuna possessed enormous *ateifuwa* or punching power. To better illustrate this point, there is interesting story told by Nagamine Shoshu (a former committee member of Shuri's Protection of Cultural Assets Department) from Kinjo-cho. It goes something like this:

In 1907, when Nagamine was about ten years old, the neighborhood of Tamaudon (the official burial place of the royal family) was the perfect spot for children to play because there were so many trees there. At that time Kiyuna Peichin was a guard at the Tamaudon and meticulously patrolled the grounds with a wooden staff that had a bell attached to its end. In between his rounds he usually took a brief rest at the guardhouse where Nagamine often saw Itosu visit and enjoy a friendly chat over a cup of tea.

With a passion for karate since childhood, Nagamine Shoshu first learned under Kiyuna. As a curious child he marvelled over watching his teacher and Itosu practice *kata* together. Kiyuna was taller than Itosu but not nearly as broad in the shoulders. Kiyuna and Itosu both had muscular arms and enormous *tako* (callouses) on their fists from relentless *makiwara* training.

As a lad, Nagamine Shoshu often heard tales about these two heroes. Such tales of heroism, exaggerated or not, have become an important part of Okinawan folklore and serve to teach valuable lessons about training and life in general. One such story surrounding the enormous punching power of Kiyuna was his problem with breaking the *makiwara* at his residence. It seemed that he could not keep a *makiwara* for more than a month because as his intensity increased he would strike it too hard, thus breaking the post. Finally, he tried tying a leather *zori* (Japanese sandal) to a tree near the Tamaudon. However, after being struck for ten days the tree died!

I would also like to impart a couple of incidents which help characterize Master Itosu. Once he tied a leather *zori* to a stone wall in an effort to build a better *makiwara*. After Itosu struck several times, the stone it was attached to ultimately gave way and pushed through the other side of the wall. After Itosu had continually relocated the *zori* in an effort to find a more solid location on which to affix it, the stone wall was destroyed.

There's another tale about Itosu defeating a fighting bull. Bullfighting dates far back into Ryukyuan history, and was particularly popular in the villages of Nakanishi and Miyagi in Urazoe. According to the old calendar, bullfighting was held every year on July 16th along with sumo wrestling and *Eisaa* (*Bon Odori* in Japanese; a festival of song, music, and dance), and attracted crowds of young and old from as far away as the suburbs of Shuri and Naha. I had the pleasure of attending the event on several occasions myself. The old tradition was discontinued sometime before the war.

On one occasion Master Itosu went to watch a bullfight with his friend. As they moved among the people, there suddenly erupted a panic, as one of the bulls broke loose and bolted through the crowd. As the panic-stricken crowd ran for cover, Itosu stood still directly before the animal. Scratching the ground with its hooves, the beast stood before Itosu snorting loudly, while tilting its enormous head down and pointing its sharp horns straight ahead. Itosu wasted no time in taking advantage and rushed at the bull, planting a powerful blow to the nose of the beast with his iron fist. Then, at the very moment the bull bolted back, Itosu clutched its horns and twisted it to the ground, whereupon the bull was captured and taken back to its pen. The crowd was overwhelmed by Itosu's unbelievable courage and skill. Although the account became a popular story of the time, it is remembered by few today.

From incidents such as these, we can deduce that two of the most powerful punchers among Bushi Matsumura's students were Kiyuna and Itosu. Yet, in spite of Itosu's diligent *makiwara* training and polished martial arts skills, I know of no episodes of him ever fighting or even having an argument throughout his entire life. Therefore, Itosu was regarded as a man of great patience, conviction, and virtue. Hence, it is because of his merit and significant contributions to the growth and direction of karate that we disciples of the art can use this *bujin* as a role model.

REVEALING THE TRUTH OF KARATE-DO

With the prefectural system replacing feudal domains in 1879, after the abolition of the Ryukyu Kingdom, Itosu retired from his position as a government official to practice and teach *to-te* at his home. In spite of political and social chaos, he remained dedicated to *to-te* and trained daily and taught diligently. Master Itosu produced many excellent students, some of whom went on to become legends themselves. If one can truly judge a teacher by his students, then Itosu Anko must be regarded as one of karate's greatest teachers.

I would like to introduce some of Master Itosu's most distinguished disciples:

Yabu Kentsu (1866–1937) was born in Shuri's Yamakawa village. Yabu was a *shihandai* (senior disciple) of Master Itosu. In 1890, he was among the first volunteers from Okinawa to enlist in the Imperial Army and went on to serve gallantly in both the Sino-Japanese and the Russo-Japanese wars, ascending to the rank of first lieutenant.

Yabu Kentsu

Funakoshi Gichin (1868–1957) was born in Shuri's Yamakawa village. In 1922, after retiring from his position as a school teacher, Funakoshi Sensei went up to Tokyo, where he devoted the rest of his life to developing and teaching karate. He is regarded by many to be the father of modern karate-do.

Funakoshi Gichin

Hanashiro Chomo (1869–1945) was born in Shuri's Yamakawa village. Hanashiro Sensei was also a *shihandai* of Master Itosu. Like Yabu Kentsu, so too was Hanashiro Sensei among the first volunteers in 1890 to enlist in the army. He courageously served in both the Sino-Japanese and Russo-Japanese wars, and like his good friend Yabu he also ascended to the rank of first lieutenant. Entering island politics after his career in the military, Hanashiro went on to become the mayor of Mawashi village.

Hanashiro Chomo

Kyan Chotoku (1870–1945) was born in Shuri's Gibo village. As a civilian, Kyan Sensei devoted his entire life to the promotion of karate-do in his tiny village.

Kyan Chotoku

Chibana Choshin (1885–1969) was born in Shuri's Torihori village. He is regarded as the founder of the Kobayashi branch of Shorin-ryu karate-do. After the war, Chibana Sensei devoted the rest of his life to developing and teaching karate-do, and was awarded the Emperor's Order of the Fourth Class.

Chibana Choshin

Tokuda Anbun (1886–1945) was born in Shuri's Sakiyama village. Tokuda Sensei worked as a regular teacher at Shuri's junior high school where he also taught karate. He died during the war in Okinawa.

Tokuda Anbun

Oshiro Chojo (1888–1939) was born in Shuri's Ounaka village. Oshiro Sensei worked as a regular teacher at the prefectural industrial high school in Okinawa. In spite of making significant contributions to karate, he is probably better known for his skills in *Yamanni-ryu bojutsu*, which he learned directly under Chinen Sanda, the best *bo* master in Okinawa at that time. It is said that Oshiro's skill with the six foot wooden staff was incomparable.

Oshiro Chojo

Mabuni Kenwa (1889–1953) was born in Shuri. After he retired from his position as a policeman, he moved to Osaka in the late twenties and devoted the rest of his life to teaching karate. Regarded as a brilliant researcher, Mabuni founded the Shito-ryu interpretation of karate-do.

Mabuni Kenwa

Gusukuma Shinpan (1890–1954) was born in Shuri's Tera village. Although employed as a regular school teacher, Gusukuma Sensei devoted all of his free time to developing and teaching karate-do.

Gusukuma Shinpan

It is clearly evident that Itosu did not act alone in his bid to modernize karate in Okinawa. The development of modern karate-do owes its thanks to the efforts of many people. Although an entire dissertation might better illuminate the magnitude of Itosu Anko's contributions to the development of modern karate-do, both in and out of Okinawa, the purpose of this presentation is only to draw your attention to it. There can be no question that Itosu Anko laid the foundation from which modern karate-do ascended.

In 1890, the military draft system was imposed upon Okinawa. Three of the first men to pass the acceptance examination were students of Itosu Anko, namely Yabu Kentsu, Hanashiro Chomo, and Kudeken Kenyu. What most impressed the army doctors about these three men during their medical examinations was their incredible physical condition. Because of this[3] to-te (karate) was under consideration to become an adjunct to the physical education curriculum of the Okinawa school systems. By April of 1901, to-te became part of the school curriculum at Shuri's Jinjo elementary school, with Itosu Sensei in charge of developing and teaching what is now described as the first building block in the foundation of modern karate.

From April of 1905, Itosu Sensei also became a part-time teacher of *to-te* at Okinawa's First Junior Prefectural High School, as well as at the Teacher's College. It was during this period that he introduced his masterpiece, five training exercises he called the *Pinan kata*.

During, and prior to, Itosu's generation such rituals as *junbi-undo* (preparatory exercises) and *kihon-undo* (fundamental exercises) were not common training practices in and around the old castle district of Shuri. In those days the *Naihanchi kata* was usually first taught to beginners. However, if children had no previous knowledge of technique and were not physically mature, this training was not considered good practice. Some systematic method of teaching *waza* (technique) was required in order for the student to progress from one level to the next. This issue weighed heavily on the mind of Master Itosu when he started teaching *to-te* to junior high school students. Hence, he created the five *Pinan kata* in an effort to introduce and familiarize beginners with the fundamental techniques of *to-te*. To this day, the *Pinan* (*Heian* in Japanese) *kata* continue to serve as the introductory platform on which much of the basics of modern karate-do rest. As such, these *kata* must be recognized as one of the greatest contributions made by Itosu Anko.

Pinan nidan

Pinan sandan

The difficulty in creating *kata* rests in such things as its intended practicality, elegance, and intellectual creativity. I am sure that Master Itosu was not able to develop such brilliant paradigms without repeated trial and error. In many ways the *Pinan* serve to remind us of his daring and the depth of his passion for *to-te*.

In October of 1908, at the age of seventy-seven, Master Itosu put brush to paper and composed the "Ten Lessons of To-te," a document outlining the *gitai* (physical and technical) value of karate. His official composition was sent to the Prefectural Ministry of Education, and his report (presented at the end of this chapter) is

Pinan yondan

Pinan yondan

regarded as an important part of the *shingitai* (mind, technique, body) principle of Okinawa karate-do, the other such document, of course, being Bushi Matsumura's "Seven Virtues of Bu," a document outlining the mind (*shin* or *kokoro*) of Okinawan karate-do.

During his lifetime Master Itosu witnessed enormous changes in Okinawa. With the *Haihan-Chiken* (the establishment of prefectures replacing feudal domains), times became difficult in old Okinawa. It was a time when the old gave way to the new, a time when the King abdicated and his kingdom was abolished. It was under those trying circumstances that Itosu Anko came to fully understand what mastering *to-te* really meant. Through the practice of *to-te*, discovering and mastering one's world within fostered an indomitable spirit and outer strength which enhanced one's understanding of life and the world without. Committed to such truth, Master Itosu resolved to dedicate the rest of his life to the practice and development of *to-te*.

There can be no question that the martial arts first ascended from man's instinct to defend himself. However, the body of moral philosophy established to govern the behavior of those who master the secrets of martial arts (called *chimugukuru* in Okinawan), elevated the discipline from a form of common brutality (killing-fist) to a sophisticated vehicle through which to enhance the living of life itself (living-fist). The annals of history are filled with the testimony of those who pursued spiritual guidance through the physical and philosophical teachings of the martial arts, leaving us with an invaluable message "there can be no end to training in the martial arts." It is in the privacy of one's own thoughts that the daily pursuit for perfection is best enjoyed.

One cannot help but admire a man like Itosu Anko, for if ever there was a model of Okinawan karate-do, it would have to be this man. His understanding of the tradition and its philosophy, and his subsequent efforts to bring it out from behind the closed doors of obscurity are, in many ways, responsible for the advent of modern karate-do. How sad it is today that so many tend to ignore that which karate truly represents. It is my greatest hope that the true elements of karate-do will one day permeate the narrow world in which the discipline presently exists. With the karate of Okinawa now being vigorously introduced the world over, we are in desperate need of ambassadors to carry the message of men like Itosu Anko.

Pinan godan

Despite living during times of great turmoil, Master Itosu never once found reason to fight with another person. He was a man of great dignity who deeply respected humanity. In many ways the fact that Itosu never fought seems to exemplify the ancient martial arts maxim *"Tatakawa zushite katsu"* (to win without fighting), which is often described as *"karate ni sente nashi"* (there is no first strike in karate).

Itosu Anko accomplished much in his long life before passing away on January 26, 1915, at the age of eighty-five. Given to him posthumously, his Buddhist name is Kenmyooin Kooen Sootoku Shinshi (meaning virtue, values, and principles) representing that for which he stood.

The Itosu family household has kept a private altar honoring the spirit of the great master for nearly a century, preserved now by his great-grandson, Itosu Ango. The family has never forgotten the impact their ancestor made on them and continue to live in perfect harmony.

Itosu Ango's printing business also contributed significantly to the development of Okinawan culture in the post-war period, and he continued to be a leading figure in the Okinawan business world as well. And if the old saying that "descendants inherit happiness from ancestors who've accumulated good deeds" is true, then it surely applies to the Itosu family. Perhaps, then, in this there is also a lesson for teachers to get back on the right path of karate-do. Gratitude knows no bounds.

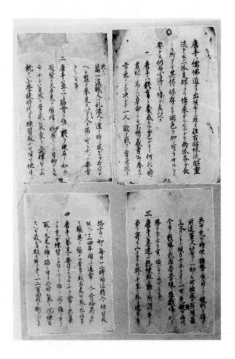

THE TEN LESSONS OF TO-TE

Karate did not descend from Buddhism or Confucianism. In the old days two schools of karate, namely the Shorin and Shorei style, were introduced from China. Both support sound principles and it is vital that they be preserved and not altered. Therefore, I will mention here what one must know about karate: Itosu Anko's "Ten Lessons of To-te," which he wrote in October of 1908.

1. Karate does not endeavor only to discipline one's physique. If and when the necessity arises to fight for a just cause, karate provides the fortitude with which to risk one's own life in support of that campaign. It is not meant to be employed against a single adversary but rather as a means of avoiding the use of one's hands and feet in the event of a potentially dangerous encounter with a ruffian or a villain.

2. The primary purpose of karate training is to strengthen the muscles, making the physique strong like iron and stone so that one can use the hands and feet to approximate such weapons as a spear or halberd. In doing so, karate training cultivates bravery and valor in children and it should be

encouraged in our elementary schools. Don't forget what the Duke of Wellington said after defeating Emperor Napoleon: "The Battle of Waterloo was won on the playing fields of Eton."

3. Karate cannot be adequately learned in a short period of time. Like a sluggish bull, regardless of how slowly it moves it will eventually cover a thousand miles. So too, for one who resolves to study diligently two or three hours every day, after three or four years of unremitting effort one's body will undergo a great transformation, revealing the very essence of karate.

4. One of the most important issues in karate is the importance of training the hands and the feet. Therefore, one must always make use of the *makiwara* in order to develop them thoroughly. In order to do this effectively, lower the shoulders, open the lungs, focus your energy, firmly grip the ground to root your posture, and sink your *ki* (the life force or intrinsic energy), forcing it into your *tanden* (area just below the navel). Following this procedure, perform one to two hundred *tsuki* (punches) with each hand every day.

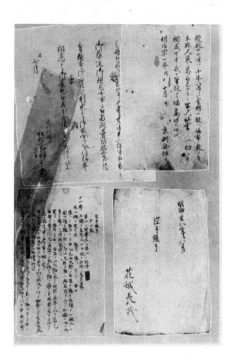

5. One must maintain an upright position in the training postures of karate. The back should be straight, loins pointing upward with the shoulders down, while maintaining a pliable power in your legs. Relax and bring together the upper and lower parts of the body with the *ki* force focused in your *tanden*.

6. Handed down by word of mouth, karate is comprised of a myriad of techniques and corresponding meanings. Resolve to independently explore the context of these techniques, observing the principles of *torite* (theory of usage), and the practical applications will be more easily understood.

7. In karate training one must determine whether the interpretation of a movement is suitable for defense or for cultivating the body.

8. Intensity is an important issue in karate training. To visualize that one is actually engaged on the battlefield during training does much to enhance progression. Therefore, the eyes should dispatch fierceness while lowering the shoulders

and contracting the body when delivering a blow. Training in this spirit prepares one for actual combat.

9. The amount of training must be in proportion to one's physical reservoir of strength and conditioning. Excessive practice is harmful to one's body and can be recognized when the face and eyes become red.

10. Participants of karate usually enjoy a long and healthy life, thanks to the benefits of unremitting training. Practice strengthens muscle and bone, improves the digestive organs, and regulates blood circulation. Therefore, if the study of karate were introduced into our (athletic) curricula from elementary school and practiced extensively we could more easily produce men of immeasurable defense capabilities.

With these teachings in mind, it is my conviction that if the students at the Shihan Chugakko (old name of Okinawa's Teachers College) practice karate they could, after graduation, introduce the discipline at the local levels; namely to elementary schools. In this way karate could be disseminated throughout the entire nation and not only benefit people in general but also serve as an enormous asset to our military forces.

—Itosu Anko
October 1908

Chapter 6

HIGAONNA KANRYO OKINA:
THE IRON-FIST WARRIOR

A DETERMINED DECADE IN CHINA

Higaonna Kanryo

After training diligently in China for ten years, Higaonna Kanryo was the man most responsible for reviving the dying practice of *chuan fa* in Naha. On April 27, 1976, I visited Higaonna Hide, a descendant of Kanryo, in Naha's Makishi village, to study his family genealogical records. According to those family records, I learned that Higaonna was the fourth son of Higaonna Kanyo, who was a ninth-generation descendant of Okinawa's Shin clan. Higaonna was born in Naha's Nishi village in 1853, the same year in which Admiral Perry visited our island. As a child, Higaonna was called Moushi. His Chinese name was Shinzen'en. Higaonna's father, Kanyo, earned a living working in the wholesale and retail business. However, transporting firewood from Kerama by a *yanbarusen* (a kind of vessel) did not furnish Higaonna Kanyo with enough money to properly educate his children.

In spite of being quite small, Higaonna was flexible and blessed with quick reflexes, which afforded him a reputation in *tegumi* (sumo) and *to-te* (karate). In 1873, when he was about twenty years old, Higaonna began training rigorously under the astute martial arts mas-

60

ter Maya Arakaki (Arakaki Seisho, 1840–1920). Responding well to his formal training, Higaonna's skill quickly improved. In fact, so outstanding did he become under the tutelage of Arakaki that he became quite well-known all around Naha. From a senior student who had trained in Fuzhou, Higaonna had heard the stories about the birthplace of *to-te* and how great the *chuan fa* was there. An ambitious and adventurous person, he longed to one day make the pilgrimage himself.

In those days the only local port from which one could journey to China was Naha. Besides serving as the official port of commerce for the government, Naha Harbor was also home to swarms of ambitious private shippers, called *touichibee*. Knowing many Chinese boats were anchored at the port of Naha, Higaonna often took his father's boat through there on business to get to know the shippers.

Ultimately, Higaonna made several friends, one of whom was a boat owner who travelled back and forth to the port of Fuzhou. After hearing of his desire to go to China, the boat owner gladly took him on. Sailing with the seasonal winds, the vessel on which Higaonna journeyed first dropped anchor at the island of Kume. Then around early March the vessel set sail for Fuzhou and under clear skies arrived at its destination in less than a week.

In spite of the assumption that Higaonna learned from Ryuryuko in Fuzhou, I would like to address Shimabukuro Kotoyu's supposition that he studied under Wai Xinxian.

Training was arduous for Higaonna in China. He was first instructed in the way of *ashi-sabaki* (stepping) and breathing techniques for four to five hours a day. Beyond that, he was responsible for weeding the garden and keeping the *dojo* floor clean at all times. As a foreigner in China, he encountered problems with learning the language and was confined to a restricted lifestyle for what seemed to him to be an eternity. Those early years were difficult for Higoanna and he often felt like returning to the Ryukyu Kingdom but he endured. When he felt homesick he sometimes thought of the poem that his *senpai* and friends composed for him when he departed from the port of Naha.

Poem:
> *Shinubi Shinubushiya Tarun Shinubushiga.*
> *Shinubaran Shinubi Sushiru Shinubi*

Interpretation:
> Anyone can be patient under ordinary circumstances.
> However real patience lies in bearing the unbearable.

When Higaonna finally learned the basic *kaishu kata* (open hand exercises) of *Sanchin, Seiyunchin,* and *Shiisouchin,* he trained so hard he often injured himself and even complained of blood in his urine. As time passed and his skills improved he was taught the more advanced *Seisan* and *Pecchurin kata.* In nearly ten years of diligent training Higaonna mastered a wide range of techniques, including the secret *keiiken,* original Chinese *chuan fa* training apparatus: *chishi* (a stick with a heavy weight on one end), *tetsurin* (iron circle), *sashi* (stone or iron hand grip), *kami* (heavy earthen jars), *sashishi* (large stone weight), and *ishi-geta* (stone clogs). Higaonna's body underwent a complete transformation in his many years of diligent study before he received his *shihandai menkyo* (master teacher license). In fact, it is said that Higaonna was in such incredible physical condition that he looked like a statue chiseled out of rock.

Although he received no formal schooling in Okinawa, no one realized the importance of a good education better than Higaonna. Hence, he diligently studied Confucianism and the tactics of Sun Tsu (fifth-century B.C. military strategist) in connection with the *chuan fa* he learned in Fuzhou. Among the many books he came to study, his favorite was the *Wubeizhi (Bubishi)* and in particular the section about the eight sayings of the fist. Through *bun bu ryo dō* (physical and philosophical as one study) Higaonna came to understand that physical training without spiritual study does not make genuine martial arts—the two are inseparable. After coming to realize the essence of martial arts, Higaonna returned to Okinawa. Although reluctant to leave his friends and his teacher, Wai Xinxian, ten years was enough time away from home, and Higaonna returned to Okinawa in his prime.

NAHA'S WELL-KNOWN "SECRET BUSHI"

In 1872 the Meiji government declared the Ryukyu Kingdom officially part of its domain, and suggested that it should conclude all relations with other countries before it could become an independent prefecture of its own. In July of 1874, the Ryukyu Administration received a special communique, dispatched from the Ministry of the Interior, directing it to adopt and institute all the Meiji regulatory policies forthwith. By December of that same year, Okinawa was ordered to sever any and all relationships with the Qing Empire, due to political friction between Qing and Japan. In spite of the Meiji government's demand that Okinawa terminate its relations with China, Okinawa continued its unofficial commerce, causing friction at both ends. Standing in opposition to the Meiji mandate was Okinawa's pro-Chinese Ishimakura political party, which itself was opposed by the Japanese Civilization party. Yet, without incident, Okinawa conformed with the establishment of the Meiji government's prefecture policy. However, in the case of Okinawa's liaison with the Middle Kingdom, the Meiji government had to dispatch an official to deal with the problem. In June of 1875, the Ministry of the Interior dispatched its emissary Matsuda Michiyuki to Okinawa to more clearly define the guidelines of its policy. In 1879, Matsuda returned with a sixth class provisional official, Ijichi Sadaka. They appeared at Shuri castle and the contents of their directive were as follows: 1) Terminate your tribute to the Qing and disregard them as your administrators; 2) Replace the Chinese calendar with the Meiji calendar (observing the Meiji Emperor); 3) Adopt the Meiji criminal justice system; 4) Reform the government to adopt Meiji policy; and 5) Send exchange students to Tokyo rather than to Beijing.

Such inflexible direction would, as the islanders saw it, destroy hundreds of years of culture, abolish a class system, its government, and depose a king. Nonetheless, in one fell swoop about 300 lords, nearly 2000 aristocratic families, and the king were deprived of their wealth and position. Then, in an effort to ensure that all foreign education was stopped, native Okinawan schools which taught Chinese philosophy, called *hira-gakko,* were replaced by Japanese Yamato schools.

In China, Higaonna grew quite despondent over the deteriorating circumstances of his homeland. His dream was to one day return to Okinawa and teach the value of martial arts training and Confucian ideals to young people. However, his dreams were shattered with the destruction of the Ryukyu Kingdom. A haunting lyric from that era, which best described the prevailing feeling among the upper class who lost their position went: *"Bunkurenaran shimachijouran, jinno-hananasachuru uchiyunatasa"* ("The world has changed and I wonder what will now happen in this new social order which places money above kingdom and class").

A popular tune then on the lips of Okinawa's Ishimakura party (who believed that the Qing would regain their strength after the Sino-Japanese War) went something like this: *"Namaya katabaruni taihoodamayarachi chiirukanno kurawademono"* ("In spite of the victory celebration at Katabaru, you should be careful because *chiirukanno* [Chinese warships] will soon be back to free us").

To say that Okinawa was at that time in complete chaos would have been an understatement. When Higaonna returned home after Okinawa's transition had taken place, he became very pessimistic knowing that things would never be restored. His pessimism grew and an intense depression ultimately led him to withdraw into the depths of Naha's Tsuji (red-light) district, to forget himself.

During that time many young people from either side of Naha

came to know who Higaonna was and, in spite of his unfortunate condition, respected his position and eagerly wanted to learn *to-te* from him. By not teaching anybody, Higaonna became well-known in the Tsuji district as a real "secret *bushi*."

There is a story about Higaonna returning home after having been out drinking at a pub in Naha's well-known red-light district when he was forty-five years old. The lady who owned the pub insisted that her servant accompany him home with a lantern because it was terribly late, very dark, and Higaonna was drunk. Together they set out for Higaonna's home but soon encountered three men just in front of the *mousuji* on Tsuji's Kushi Street. One of the three men who lay waiting for the drunken victim yelled out, "Hey its the old Bushi Higaonna!" The second man quickly kicked the lantern out of the servant's hand while the third drove a punch directly into the center of Higaonna's stomach. Intoxicated, but not incapacitated, Higaonna slid back just an inch as the fist tried to find its mark and drove his iron-like knuckles deeply into the wrist of the assailant. The man let out a terrible scream and ran in desperation to the theater across the street, with the other two following closely behind.

I heard about this incident from my senior in Tomari, Iha no Aji Tanmei. He used to be the manager of that theater. The man who had tried to attack Higaonna was no one other than Sakuma Kanta, an unrivaled street fighter in Tsuji. Sakuma later said that he ran away because he thought his wrist had been broken in several places by Higaonna's surprise counter punch. During that time, Sakuma was considered equal to Motobu Saru (Motobu Choki). Iha no Aji Tanmei also told me that the theater often presented stories about local heroes and brave *bujin*.

Interested in such things, Higaonna happened to come to the theater one evening. After the performance Iha invited Higaonna backstage and remembered him smiling and being quite modest. "I'll never forget what the great master maintained about martial arts," said Iha: "Although there may be many techniques during any encounter, one blow can determine its outcome. Your life may rest on how well your fist is prepared. The saying *"I ken no kon"* means "Train one fist to penetrate the spirit." This is the essence of a *Bushi*. Iha maintained that he learned Higaonna's lesson by heart and often used his words as part of the plays at the theater.

THE RESTORER OF NAHA-TE

Just the title of this sub-chapter alone, "The Restorer of Naha-te," is meant to portray someone who was deeply concerned with awakening the fighting traditions once vigorously practiced in and around the old district of Naha.

After the abolition of the Ryukyu Kingdom and the establishment of Okinawa Prefecture, its socialist government, and the Japanese school system, everyday life on the island, in spite of lingering political animosity, finally resumed without presenting ungovernable difficulties.

As I have previously mentioned, Okinawa initiated a military draft system in 1890 in which Yabu Kentsu, Hanashiro Chomo, and Kudeken Kenyu were among the very first karate men to pass the acceptance exam. These men owed their physical conditioning to diligent training in karate. All were very muscular and stood over five-feet, seven- or eight-inches tall. The military doctors at their medical examinations were overwhelmed and wondered just how they forged such bodies of steel? After interviewing each of the men, it was discovered that such conditioning was the result of methodical training in martial arts. Deeply impressed, the doctors rapidly encouraged such training and made an application to have the practice become part of military training. That resulted in karate gaining public attention and becoming a popular practice among young people. The three men distinguished themselves in combat, which resulted in them becoming non-commissioned officers. Both Yabu and Hanashiro went on to become regarded as authorities of karate during their time and were responsible for influencing the growth and direction of the art in Okinawa.

With the practice brought out from behind the closed doors of seclusion, many young men in Naha interested in learning *to-te* went to Higaonna for instruction. Although the actual reason he finally taught Chinese *chuan fa* remains the subject of some curiosity, Higaonna, in spite of having remained despondent for so long, ultimately accepted a following and was regarded as the man most responsible for reviving the dormant fighting arts in and around the district of Naha.

From just after the turn of the twentieth century, Higaonna Kanryo personally trained such men as Kyoda Juhatsu (1887–1968), Miyagi Chojun (1888–1953), and Shiroma Koki (nd). Described as *to-te* in Okinawa, the *chuan fa* that Higaonna

Kyoda Juhatsu

Miyagi Chojun

taught during that golden era became such a popular practice that by 1927 it actually became known as Naha-to-te or simply Naha-te.[5]

Perhaps one of Higaonna's best-known disciples was Miyagi Chojun, the man who founded the Goju karate tradition. Miyagi spent his whole life pursuing the deepest understanding of karate-do. Kyoda Juhatsu was another disciple of Higaonna who, in spite of being a teacher for most of his life, also devoted his life to the art and founded the Toon[6] School of Karate-do. Gusukuma Koki, yet another of Higaonna's disciples, became a Christian and dedicated the rest of his life to serving God.

There is an interesting account of a journalist from the Japanese mainland who, after watching Higaonna's young students demonstrate the *Sanchin kata,* was deeply impressed by the way in which they moved their hips, contracted their muscles, and breathed. The following haiku[7] was composed by that journalist.

Haiku:
Toshu kuken hatsukaminari wo toriosou

Translation:
A roll of thunder, seizing the first bolt of lightning with the empty hands.

When Higaonna taught *to-te jutsu,* he was known to always cite passages from the ancient book of Chinese martial arts called the *Wubeizhi,* a document perhaps better known by its Japanese pronunciation, *Bubishi.*[8] Underscoring chuan fa's[9] eight precepts, and the strategy of Sun Tsu, Higaonna maintained that physical training without moral philosophy was not *to-te.*

When Miyagi Chojun, Higaonna's most prolific disciple, became associated with Kyoto's prestigious Dai Nippon Butokukai (Japan's eminent Association of Martial Virtues) in 1930, it was required that he register his *ryuha* (systematized fighting tradition) in the same way other codified disciplines had done for generations. In Okinawa, karate had only been referred to as *to-te jutsu* until 1927, after which it was categorized as Naha-te, Shuri-te, and Tomari-te. Always moved by the way Higaonna described the importance of chuan fa's eight precepts, Miyagi Sensei selected a fitting term from the chapter's third passage to describe his interpretation of Naha-te. The passage reads: *"Howa Goju o donto su"* (Inhaling represents softness/exhaling represents hardness), and the term Goju (hard/soft) became the official name describing the tradition that Miyagi Sensei went on to propagate. That was the birth of Goju-ryu and little did Miyagi Sensei ever know just how significant that name would become.

Younger days of Miyagi (left) and Kyoda (right).

Higaonna Kanryo passed away on December 15th, 1917. He was loved like a father by his students. Yet his spirit remains through the teachings he passed down and his name will live on forever in the annals of karate. Higaonna Kanryo was the man most responsible for breathing life back into a neglected tradition in and around the district of Naha at the dawn of this century.

第Ⅱ図

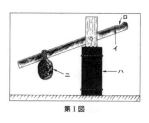

第Ⅰ図

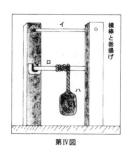

第Ⅳ図

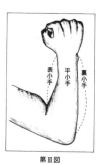

第Ⅲ図

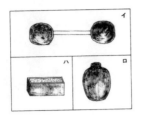

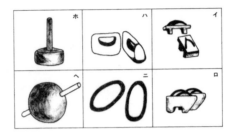

HIGAONNA'S ADVICE FOR USING SUPPLEMENTARY EQUIPMENT IN KARATE-DO

The following training advice has been passed down from Higaonna Kanryo:

• The results of one's effort are cumulative: never rush or show off.
• Train in accordance with your ability.
• Repeat each exercise until exhaustion and build intensity gradually.

Higaonna Kanryo believed so deeply in "The Eight Precepts of Chuan Fa" that I would like to conclude the section on him by introducing them. [They appear here as they do in Patrick McCarthy's English translation of the *Bubishi*]:

1. The human mind is one with heaven and earth.
2. Our blood circulation is systemically similar to the solar and lunar cycles of each day.
3. Inhaling represents softness while exhaling characterizes hardness.
4. Adapt to changing conditions.
5. Response must result without conscious thought.
6. Combative engagement distance and posture dictates the meeting.
7. See what is unseeable.
8. Expect what is unexpected.

Chapter 7

FUNAKOSHI GICHIN SENSEI: FIRST PROPAGATOR OF KARATE-DO

REFUSING TO REMOVE HIS TOPKNOT

The only son of Funakoshi Gisu, Funakoshi Gichin Sensei was born on November 10, 1868, to a *kemochi* (aristocratic) family in Shuri's Yamakawa village. However, according to the family register, Gichin was born in 1870, not 1868. Because he desired to become a doctor, Funakoshi falsified the year of his birth because applicants for medical school needed to be born after 1870.

Born prematurely, Funakoshi was quite small and weak as a child. His family was afraid that he would not live past the age of three. Because of this, his parents

Funakoshi Gichin

and grandparents took extra good care of him as a child. His health and well-being were the first priority of his family. Fortunately, he never suffered health problems during his childhood.

Because of his childhood friendship with the first son of Azato Anko, a revered master of karate, Gichin was introduced to the discipline at a very early age. Master Azato was not only familiar with empty-hand fighting, but also excelled in horsemanship and Japanese fencing. Moreover, Azato Sensei was a brilliant scholar who, in

Funakoshi's mind, exemplified the perfect *bujin:* not only brave but also intelligent. Funakoshi Sensei was truly fortunate to have found such a noble teacher so early in his life. Being trained by an excellent teacher is essential to the development of any martial artist.

From before he could barely comprehend them, Funakoshi unrelentingly read *The Four Chinese Classics* and the five *Confucian Classics,* under the strict guidance of his grandfather. Coupled with his devotion to *to-te jutsu* under the tutelage of Master Azato, Funakoshi also diligently studied calligraphy.

As was often the case with his generation, described as the "old days," karate training was done in the early morning, and much emphasis was placed on understanding the common principles on which karate rested while developing a considerable foundation. It took virtually several years of diligent practice to completely learn a single *kata,* unlike today's pointless, but popular, accumulation of many *kata* in a brief time. A student continued training until his master chose to introduce the next level of material, not the other way around. There were no commercial *dojo* in those days either, and students had to be enthusiastic or they were not accepted by teachers in the first place.

The study of karate in those days, unlike today, emphasized the balance of physical training with moral education to form a single tradition. *Budo* (martial ways) was "the Way" through which men developed bravery and intellect, which underscored the essence of the ancient discipline. Unlike the adversarial training of sport karate today, where winning is the focal point of practice, practitioners of Funakoshi's generation strived solely to overcome a more ominous enemy: the self. Compared to that which lay behind or ahead of the *deshi* (disciple), nothing was more important than that which lay within. To this end, the *sensei* gave completely of himself, forming an inseparable spiritual bond with his *deshi.*

It wasn't until 1879 that Okinawa was officially established as an independent prefecture, replacing the Ryukyu Kingdom's status as a feudal domain of the Satsuma. During the time that Funakoshi was born, the momentum of the Meiji Restoration was already well under way with two political factions, the Enlightenment Coalition and the Obstinate Party arguing over the *chongmage* (topknot hair style) issue: "Should men continue to sport their feudal hair fashion or not?" With the Funakoshi family supporting the Obstinate Party's conviction that a *chongmage* was not just a sign of maturity and virility, but a symbol of manhood itself, Funakoshi was not permitted to remove his topknot. In order to be accepted at medical school in Tokyo during that time, students had to adhere strictly to the modern standards. In spite of this matter not being terribly important by today's standards, it was, nonetheless, an issue of some magnitude then. Ultimately, Funakoshi did cut off his *chongmage*, but not before forfeiting his chance to go to medical school. Subsequently, he worked for an elementary school as an assistant teacher.

TOKYO: THE FOUNDATION UPON WHICH JAPANESE KARATE-DO WAS BUILT

In 1888, after he had become a school teacher and was wearing his hair acceptably short, Funakoshi made a special trip to the house of his parents to reveal his new image. In addition to his new hair style, he was also dressed in a Western-style suit, which not only shocked his parents but infuriated his father. "Shame on you!," his father yelled. "You are a disgrace to the family of a *kemochi*." So distressed was Funakoshi's mother that she ran out the back door because she could not look at his face. Comparing such things to what is taken for granted in today's generation, it is interesting to understand the mind-set during those days.

In teaching school for about thirty years, Funakoshi always worked in the neighborhoods of Shuri and Naha. There he was able to continue his training under both Azato and Itosu Anko. I remember an occasion in 1916, when I was in the third grade. There was a public sports day for elementary schools in Naha at Onoyama Park. Funakoshi Sensei had been teaching at Tomari Elementary School at that time. He taught the *Naihanchi* and *Pinan kata* to boys of grades three and beyond. Later, more than 200 boys performed a group demonstration of *kata*. It is as clear to me now as it was then. I remember the big mole on Funakoshi's forehead, and we brat kids calling it *"bushi aja,"* maintaining that only real *bushi* had such a mark.

It was in 1912 that the Imperial First Fleet, under the command of Admiral Dewa, first anchored at Nakagusuku Bay. Ten sailors and a couple of commissioned officers were selected to stay and study karate under Funakoshi Sensei for about one week at the prefectural junior high school. That seemed to indicate karate was beginning to be noticed in Tokyo.

Later, in 1921, Prince (the future Emperor) Hirohito visited Okinawa en route to Europe. We were all very excited that someone so dignified was coming to Okinawa. In fact, the commander of the ship bearing the prince was an Okinawan, a certain Lieutenant (later Captain) Kanna Kenwa. It was probably because karate was our native martial art that a demonstration of it was chosen to be presented before the prince. The presentation was held in front of the main building at Shuri Castle. Put in charge of organizing the demonstration, Funakoshi wrote, in his biography, that this demonstration was a very honorable day in his life.

Toward the end of 1921, the *Monbusho* (Ministry of Education) began planning the first *Kobujutsu-Taiiku-Tenrankai*

The main building of Shuri Castle.

(Athletic Exhibition of Ancient Martial Arts) in Tokyo. Okinawa prefecture decided to take part in this milestone event and petitioned Funakoshi Sensei. With the Okinawan Prefectural Board of Education knowing Funakoshi to be intelligent, a reputable teacher, and expert in karate, he was an excellent candidate to present the local tradition before the rest of the nation.

Having retired from his teaching position at that time, Funakoshi Sensei gladly accepted the offer, believing that it was the perfect opportunity to introduce karate to the nation. In preparing for his demonstration, Funakoshi realized that any demonstration given without an accompanying explanation of the inner-workings of the discipline might puzzle those who did not have a preliminary knowledge of our unique art of self-defense. In an effort to provide supplementary information, Funakoshi provided pictures for his exhibition characterizing how to move the body and use the hands in karate along with an explanation of *kata* and *kumite* written on two scrolls. His undertaking was successful and that presentation is now regarded as the first official demonstration of karate in the heart of Japan.

Although he had expected to return home to Okinawa soon after the exhibition was over, Funakoshi was asked to stay on and lecture on karate here and there. Realizing what his presence in the nation's capital actually meant for the future direction of karate, Funakoshi deeply pondered his course of action. "My responsibility to karate and our nation far exceeds my own personal interests. Recognizing my obligation, I cannot return home without first completing this mission." Hence, Funakoshi Sensei decided to remain in Tokyo, and the foundation of modern Japanese karate-do was set in motion.

Funakoshi Sensei found meager but friendly accommodations at the *Meisei-juku* in Tokyo's Koishikawa district. The *Meisei-juku* was a dormitory for Okinawan students and while Funakoshi Sensei was staying there he was permitted to use the hall as a makeshift *dojo*. However, in spite of being a karate *shihan* he was not receiving any income from his teachings. With only little money and no financial assistance, Funakoshi Sensei was really starting his new life from scratch.

In a spirit of great resolve, Funakoshi expressed his feelings in a poem he composed:

Poem:
> *Nankai no shingi kore kuken*
> *Uramubeshi suibi seiden o tatsu*
> *Tareka tsukuran chuko taisei no waza*
> *Konokokoro funbatsushite soten ni chikou*

Translation:
> In the South Seas there exists a wonderful
> method of using the empty hands.
> It's too bad, however, that this tradition has declined.
> I wonder who can successfully revive this great art?
> I swear before heaven that I will make every effort
> to re-cultivate this spirit.

Funakoshi was truly a man of inner strength! What self-confidence and humility! In spite of his position, his everyday life was quite severe. He lived in the tiny dormitory's three-mat reception room, worked as the maintenance man and kept the garden, and had to pay rent like any other student. His main duties included cleaning the dormitory, as well as collecting and distributing the mail delivery to each student's room. Funakoshi Sensei divided his time in an effort to teach karate to those interested in learning the art. Of course, there were not so many students in those days and he sometimes ran short of money, which often resulted in his having to go without food. During those adverse times he even went to pawnshops to hawk personal belongings in an effort to survive.

To help explain what karate was, and promote the foreign tradition, Funakoshi published *Ryukyu Kenpo To-te* (The Chinese Art of Chuan Fa from Ryukyu) in 1922. Because of the growing interest a second revised edition, titled *Retan Goshin To-te Jutsu,* was published in 1925. It included photographs and additional text along with the revised title. Funakoshi's personal circumstances improved as a result. Through word of mouth, his classes, in a just a couple of years, steadily increased. In fact, Funakoshi's teaching ultimately generated a following large enough that he was able to establish a karate *kenkyukai* (research society) at Keio University, one of the most prestigious academic institutions in the entire country. This was the very first karate club in Tokyo.

When the *Meisei-juku* was renovated to accommodate the Okinawan Scholarship Association, Funakoshi had to relocate his *dojo*. Fortunately, the prominent swordsman and master of kendo Nakayama Hakudo offered Funakoshi the use of his own *dojo* in Hongo-Yumi-cho during the times when it was unoccupied. Nakayama's *dojo* had a reputation for being the very best in the nation, and his offer of its use was more than Funakoshi could have ever expected.

Although there has never been much written about his relationship with Nakayama Hakudo, it had, nonetheless, played an instrumental role in bringing Funakoshi's campaign to the forefront of public recognition. With Nakayama having such an influential school, many prominent people studied there and came to know about the karate classes that Funakoshi taught. Master Nakayama encouraged many members to support Funakoshi's movement by telling their friends about his new classes. Nakayama's *dojo* became much more diverse with Funakoshi teaching karate there, which in many ways enhanced the public image of his school. However, and more important, allowing Funakoshi to teach there was, in the public eye, the sword master's seal of approval. In those days, for a teacher of martial arts to receive an endorsement from someone like Nakayama Hakudo was quite an accomplishment, to say the very least.

After moving into the second floor of a house in Nakayama's neighborhood, Funakoshi began to teach at the enormous *dojo* and soon attracted hordes of students. For the lonely school teacher from Okinawa, a new dawn illuminated the darkness of his lengthy hardships. From that time and through the new contacts he made, Funakoshi Sensei was invited to local universities and ultimately established sizable followings at universities such as Waseda, Hosei, Nihon Medical, Todai, Shodai, and Nodai.

In 1935, the ideograms describing *to-te* (Chinese hand) were officially changed to read karate-do (empty-hand way), and Funakoshi Sensei used the new term when he published his next book, titled *Karate-do Kyohan*. By 1936, as karate grew more and more popular, Funakoshi Sensei became quite well known and had taken on many new students. In fact, because his student population grew to such a size and he could only teach at the Nakayama *dojo* when it was unoccupied, Funakoshi Sensei began looking for another location in which to teach. However, rather than bother Mr. Nakayama, his executive members organized "a *dojo* establishment committee" for Funakoshi in an effort to collect enough money to start his own *dojo*.

The idea was disclosed to karate enthusiasts all over Japan and, remarkably, more than enough money was collected for the purpose. Funakoshi Sensei must have been very gratified to have experienced the fruit of such labor. In the spring of 1938, the *dojo* of his longing, the Shotokan, was built in Tokyo's Zoshigaya Toshima-ward. This was the birth of the eminent Shotokan karate *dojo*.

The Shotokan was the first professional karate *dojo* in the nation and Funakoshi Sensei was seventy years old at this time. After it was built, new students flocked to the school day by day. As time passed and Funakoshi learned what it took to smoothly operate a profession-al school, *dojo* rules were established, teaching guidelines were set up, and grade requirements were created. In an effort to take some of the burden off his shoulders, Funakoshi Sensei later appointed his son, Gigo, to be his assistant at the Shotokan.

In addition to teaching at the Shotokan, Funakoshi Sensei also continued to teach at several universities in Tokyo. After graduation, each university student who had become proficient in karate-do intro-duced the art on returning back to his own hometown. Hence, karate-do found its way from the nation's capital into the tiny rural districts of Japan.

Unfortunately, Funakoshi's dream was destroyed during the attack on Tokyo in 1945, when the Shotokan was burned to the ground. The product of Funakoshi's life was reduced to ashes, and, according to his biography, he was bitterly disappointed at the end of war.

SPENDING HIS LIFE PROPAGATING KARATE-DO

While Funakoshi was alive, I enjoyed the opportunity of being in the same room with him on many occasions. I remember Funakoshi Sensei, a small man of approximately five feet, always sat up on two cushions on the tatami floor. On the many occasions that I saw him he always wore a Japanese kimono rather than Western clothes, he was emotionally steady and was never content to be second best. He believed very deeply that if one trained diligently enough one could achieve that which one desired. In those days, during the rainy season, Japanese people usually wore very high clogs to avoid getting their feet wet. However, even on fine days, Funakoshi Sensei wore high-style clogs, insisting that he was just training. "I don't wear them for show," maintained Funakoshi, "a disciple of budo must train his legs and col-lect energy in the lower abdomen always."

It was very motivating for me to see such spirit in such a small body. Funakoshi Sensei was truly a remarkable person, a man who exemplified what it meant to be a martial artist.

Funakoshi Gichin's Twenty Principles of Karate-do.

FUNAKOSHI SENSEI'S TWENTY PRINCIPLES OF KARATE-DO

1. Never forget that karate begins and ends with courtesy.
2. There is no first attack in karate.
3. Karate cultivates self-esteem.
4. First know yourself, before trying to understand others.
5. Spirit before technique.
6. Respond with an unfettered mind.
7. Do not dwell on misfortune.
8. Don't believe that karate training is restricted only to the *dojo*.
9. Karate is a lifelong pursuit.
10. When you learn how karate is related to everyday life, you will have discovered its essence.
11. Karate is like hot water, if its heat is removed it becomes cold.
12. Rather than worrying about winning, think about not losing.
13. Change your tactics according to your opponent's movements.

14. The outcome of any fight depends on dominating both protected and unprotected areas.

15. Think of your hands and feet as swords.

16. When you go out it is best to act as if you had a million enemies waiting for you.

17. Fixed stances are important for beginners until natural postures become second nature.

18. In spite of actual fighting always being different, the principles of *kata* never change.

19. Don't forget about the strength and weakness of your power, how to stretch and contract your muscles, and the proper execution of technique.

20. Constantly think about improvement.

Sometime before Funakoshi Sensei built the Shotokan, Kano Jigoro, the founder of judo, asked him to establish a karate section within the judo Kodokan. However, Funakoshi politely declined, believing that while it may indeed have facilitated the development of karate, he did not think that the tradition should be subject to, or conform with, the practice of judo. Funakoshi believed that karate should be equal when compared to other Japanese martial arts. In many ways, it was because of his unswerving conviction that karate-do, the humble tradition of Okinawa, became not only a martial art equal to other martial arts in Japan, but one of the most popular fighting traditions throughout the world.

Yet, in understanding the impact that Funakoshi Sensei had on the advent and subsequent development of modern karate-do, I must humbly draw the reader's attention to several important historical facts in an effort to avoid confusion about our cultural tradition.

Okinawan karate evolved from generations of synthesizing, re-interpreting, and codifying both Chinese and indigenous Okinawan self-defense principles. After Funakoshi had already introduced karate in Tokyo under the name Ryukyu *kempo to-te jutsu* (the Ryukyuan Chinese self-defense art of *chuan fa*), Okinawan public officials were obliged to establish a name which might better reveal its native history rather than divulging its foreign influence, because of Japan's position with China. Once known as "*te*" (literally hand, but referring to the art of self-defense), karate became known as the "*te*" traditions of Shuri, Naha, and Tomari: thus Shuri-te, Naha-te, and Tomari-te. In an effort to provide a more suitable name, Funakoshi vigorously cultivated the new term "karate-do" ("empty-hand way") and used Japanese pronunciations in place of the Chinese/Okinawan names when describing the many *kata* he taught. As an Okinawan, and a karate research historian dedicated to preserving the value of our profound cultural tradition, I believe very strongly that the original names should not be lost or misplaced. If we continue to ignore the original names we will most certainly lose the cultural identity of our tradition.

In his 1956 book, *Karate-do My Way My Life,* Funakoshi wrote that the "names of *kata* were a little bit difficult for the Japanese to understand because they were either pronounced in the Okinawan dialect or in Chinese. Moreover," Funakoshi continued, "some [flowery!!] *kata* simply did not fit into Japanese [martial arts] culture." Name changes included Ryukyu *kempo to-te jutsu*, now described as *koryu* (ancient), and changed to *karate-do* (empty-hand way). In the case of *kata, Pinan* was changed to be pronounced *Heian; Naihanchi* was changed to *Tekki; Passai* was changed to *Bassai; Wanshu* was changed to *Enpi; Rohai* was changed to *Meikyo; Chinto* was changed to *Gankaku; Kusanku* was changed to *Kanku; Useishi* was changed to *Gojushiho; Seisan* was changed to *Hangetsu;* and so on.

Proud of our cultural heritage, and considering the present-day positive Japan/China relations, I feel very strongly about having the names of the *kata* being changed back to what they should be. In that way a very important part of karate tradition will finally be restored.

Among the physical characteristics that were inappropriately altered under Funakoshi's direction was the *nekoashi dachi* (cat stance). The *nekoashi dachi* originally represented a transitory posture through which to avoid an attack, or to pull someone off balance, after which a subsequent technique could be performed. By changing the *nekoashi dachi* into the longer *kokutsu dachi* (back stance), the original application to which it applies cannot be employed, and the rhythm of the *kata* is therefore altered. Moreover, this has also generated a completely new tradition where one was not needed.

Historically, it remains clear that "*kata* should never be changed; it is inappropriate." If someone wants to create their own *kata,* that is that person's own business. However, I believe that it is wrong to consciously alter a classical tradition just to meet the needs of a different culture, or for any reason, for that matter.

When considering the initial stages of Funakoshi's effort to introduce and popularize *to-te jutsu* (a Chinese-based tradition) on the mainland of Japan during a period of intense anti-Chinese sentiment and escalating militarism, I can well understand the problems that he faced. Okinawans were not so highly respected in *Yamato* (pure Japanese) society; hence, it was probably difficult enough just to introduce karate alone without focusing on the culture from which it came. With that in mind, we must therefore consider what Funakoshi did a brilliant maneuver, especially if we are to measure the end result; "the end justifies the means!" Under those chaotic and inflexible circumstances Funakoshi had no alternative if karate was to be accepted but to comply with cultural forces or simply be rejected. Foreign readers should be interested to learn an important maxim in Japanese culture which states: *"Derukugi wa utareru,"* or "a protruding nail gets hammered down." This old maxim aptly describes anyone different in Japanese society; they conform or are methodically ostracized.

Notwithstanding, we must acknowledge Funakoshi Gichin's enormous contributions to the advent and development of modern karate-do and respect his diligent efforts. And, while he did not invent the discipline, it remains obvious why he has been perceived as the "Father of Modern Karate-do."

In memory of this great master, two stone monuments were erected on December 1, 1968, at the famous Enkaku-ji temple in Kita-Kamakura by Funakoshi's loyal students. Etched in stone, one reads *"Karate ni sente nashi"* (there is no first attack in karate), and was chiseled by Asahina Sogen, the priest in charge of the temple. The other, etched by Ohama Nobuhide, reads:

Funakoshi Gichin Sensei, of karate-do, was born the 10th of June 1870, in Shuri Okinawa. From about eleven years old he began to study *to-te jutsu* under Azato Anko and Itosu Anko. He practiced diligently and in 1912 became the president of the Okinawan Shobukai. In May of 1922, he relocated to Tokyo and became a professional teacher of karate-do. He devoted his entire life to the development of karate-do. He lived out his eighty-eight years of life and left this world on April 26, 1957.

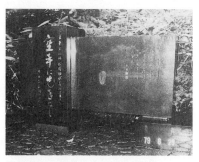

The stone monument etched to Funakoshi Gichin by Ohama Nobuhide.

Reinterpreting *to-te jutsu*, the Sensei promulgated karate-do while not losing its original philosophy. Like *bugei* (classical martial arts), so too is the pinnacle of karate *"mu"* (enlightenment): to purify and make one empty through the transformation from *"jutsu"* to *"do."* Through his famous words *"Karate ni sente nashi"* (there is no first attack in karate) and *"Karate wa kunshi no bugei"* (karate is the martial art of intelligent people), Sensei helped us to better understand the term *"jutsu."* In an effort to commemorate his virtue and great contributions to modern karate-do as a pioneer, we, his loyal students, organized the Shotokai and erected this monument at the Enkakuji. *"Kenzen-ichi"* ("The fist and Zen are one").

The establishment of these monuments was a meaningful contribution to world karate history, and also to the Okinawan people. Bringing this chapter to an end, I would like to conclude with a final word about Master Funakoshi.

He died at the age of eighty-eight after living a long and productive life. Weak and frail as a child, he was not expected to live past about the age of three. However, though diligent training while observing the principles of karate-do, he cultivated both a strong body and indomitable spirit, never getting sick a day in his long life. Starting with nothing, Funakoshi Sensei was fifty years old when he first went to Tokyo. After years of relentless effort, and in spite of opposition, Funakoshi Gichin established a foundation strong enough to support the weight of his enormous campaign. Devoting his entire life to the development, preservation, and promotion of karate-do, he overcame his early difficulties in Tokyo. While not actually the inventor of the art, Funakoshi Gichin was principally responsible for the development of modern karate-do in Japan. The achievements of this great man will remain in the annals of karate forever, and I cannot help but deeply respect him and his efforts.

Chapter 8

KYAN CHOTOKU SENSEI:
A TINY MAN WITH A SELF-TRAINED
FIGHTING SPIRIT

THE LESSON OF A STRICT FATHER

Kyan Chotoku was born in December of 1870 in Shuri's Gibo village. The son of a very strict father, Kyan Chofu, their family were descendants of Shoen, and related to Shoshi-O (1497–1555), the fourth king of the old Ryukyu kingdom. Employed by Shotai-O (1843–1901), the last king of the Ryukyu kingdom, Chofu was responsible for the keeping of the royal *hanko* (official seal of the king) and was schooled in the study of ancient Japanese and Chinese culture and thought. Moreover, Chofu was

Kyan Chotoku

also regarded as a scholar warrior, a man who was well trained in the fighting traditions and equally recognized for his intellect.

Leaving Okinawa for nearly four years, from the age of twelve to age sixteen, young Chotoku resided in Tokyo with his father, where he studied *Kangaku* (the study of Chinese culture and thought) at the *Nishogakusha*. Being born a descendant of royalty meant that Chotoku was destined to walk in the footsteps of his ancestors. Since as a child Chotoku was smaller and weaker than his father, his years in Tokyo were also spent diligently pursuing karate and jujutsu training.

Sometime around the year 1932, I was working at the Kadena police station. The head of that station in those days was a man named Hiyago Anko. I remember Mr. Hiyago once telling me a story about when Kyan and his father lived in Tokyo. The father of Hiyago Anko, like Kyan's father, had also once been employed by the Sho family and was a former *peichin*. When it got cold in Tokyo, Hiyago Anko and his brothers often snuggled together under the *kotatsu* (a table covered by a quilt to contain the heat source from underneath) to keep warm. Whenever they did this, Hiyago's father would scold them by saying "You are the sons of a *peichin*, don't be such cowards! Did you know that Chotoku and his father always train outside on such miserable days?"

After Kyan Chofu completed his assignment in Tokyo, the Kyans returned to Okinawa and lived between Shuri and Mawashi in Naha's Takaraguchi district. One day not long after their return, Chotoku stood in front of the altar in their living room listening to his father. "You're small but have a competitive spirit, Chotoku," said his father. "Even though you do not have the body of a martial artist, you can still develop effective technique depending entirely on how diligently you train yourself. You can be second to none," his father continued, "if you develop the technique suitable for a person of your body size, and master the application of the *kata*."

There was a famous seventeenth-century general named Kabayama Hisataka who served the Shimazu warriors in Satsuma. He gained the nickname "Oni-Shogun" (Devil General) at the battle of Keicho, and he, too, was quite small like Kyan—only about five shaku (150 cm). However, in spite of his tiny size he was regarded as a bold hero. In fact, so fierce was Kabayama that people of that era often said that trying to defeat him was like trying to swallow a needle.

Often when one first becomes strong through karate training, one can become arrogant and develop into a show-off. It is very important for one to transcend this affliction. If one is to truly understand the fighting traditions and become a *bujin* (person dedicated to martial arts) they must first embrace Matsumura's "Seven Virtues of *Bu:*"

1) forbid willful violence
2) govern the warrior
3) fortify people
4) foster virtue
5) appease the community

6) bring about a general harmony . . .

7) and prosperity

In the ancient words of his predecessors, handed down in a poem, Kyan's father willed him the following verse and asked Kyan to never forget to the value of its contents.

Poem:
> Chichishi no ishiji toimamuteuriba
> Noyodesukunayuga kamin shimun

Interpretation:
> Accomplishment is not limited to rank or position, and
> can be realized by everyone. How can you ever fail if
> you maintain a serious commitment to be prudent?

Back home, Kyan ultimately studied under such great masters as Bushi Matsumura Sokon and Itosu Anko in Shuri, and Oyadomari Kokan in Tomari. He became so devoted to pursuing the fighting traditions in and around the districts of Shuri and Tomari that he finally transcended his weakness, and learned how to use his tiny body to overcome a larger opponent. Often caught with his back to the wall, Kyan popularized innovative ways of escaping injury by moving laterally rather than moving forward or backward.

Once he discovered the importance of shifting and moving his small body to gain a superior position in an effort to subjugate an opponent, he focused his training on *ashi-sabaki* (footwork), and often trained down at the riverside, or sometimes on the back of a bridge railing. Within a few years of training, Kyan mastered the secret essence of karate by reinterpreting its principles and applying them to his small body. In fact, so diligently did Kyan practice karate that, by the time he turned thirty years old, he was well known in and around Shuri and Naha by the Okinawan name of "Chan Mi-Gwa" (Small Eye Kyan).

During the establishment of the *haihanchiken* (prefectures replacing feudal domains) most *kemochi* (aristocratic families) lost both their position and stipend. The Kyan family was among those who were affected by the transition and knew only hard times after that. A biting poem describes a feeling prevalent during that time.

Poem:
> Ugade nachikasaya haiban no samure
> meetariyakante umaguwa sunchi

Interpretation:

Before the Haihanchiken Ryukyu Kemochi strut about. Now, however, after losing both their position, and stipend, they have been reduced to hiding their faces under their hats as coachmen pulling carts. It's a pity to see them.

I can imagine that Kyan Sensei grew up knowing only too well what hard times really meant. Finally, and for financial reasons, Kyan Sensei had to relocate to Makihara in Yomitan village. As a descendant of the Sho family he was still privileged to some inheritance and got use of a small plot of land located in Makihara, handed down by the Sho family. Cultivating silkworms and hauling a cart, Kyan was able to carve out a meager existence. Yet, in spite of his difficult times, he never once gave up his practice of martial arts. It was during that time that Kyan Sensei learned the *Kusanku kata* from Master Yara of Chatan.

Known in the history of karate as Chatan Yara, he was a public official who was sent to Nakagami-Yomitan by the Sho administration to manage their private riding stables in Makihara. In spite of being younger than Matsumura Sokon, Yara was certainly not inferior to him in technique and was regarded as a prominent *bujin* by all those who knew him.

Kyan Sensei often talked about Chatan Yara to his student Arakaki Ankichi. This I know because Arakaki Sensei told me directly. According to him, Chan Mi-Gwa once said that "When Yara was young, he developed remarkable agility and had really powerful legs." One story maintained that in his youth he once jumped off one end of the Hijabashi (Hija bridge) and then leaped back up the other side like a bird in flight. However, when Kyan learned from him, his strength had declined considerably and he needed a stick for walking about.

One evening while Kyan Sensei was lecturing a couple of students in his yard, he swung his walking stick around and abruptly shoved it at Arakaki's chest and asked how he might handle such an encounter. Ankichi Sensei told me that Chan Mi-Gwa, in spite of his age, was still quite intense, and that his stable posture controlled his very *maai* (distance), which resulted in Arakaki's inability to respond at all. All he could do was break out into a cold sweat after being provoked by Master Kyan.

Up until that time Arakaki had been somewhat of a braggart because he had quite a positive opinion of his own skills. However, the old master really hit home with his precision. He always maintained that well-trained *bujin* always had something which transcended age and physical technique. There was no question that Kyan Sensei, in his lifetime of training, had established powerful *ki* energy. So impressed was he with Master Kyan's skill, that Arakaki Sensei trained even harder from that point on.

Deeply moved after hearing that story from Arakaki Sensei, I also intensified my resolve to train even harder. The *Kusanku kata* was the principal vehicle through which Yara transmitted the secret applications of karate to Kyan. Kyan taught it to Arakaki, who taught it to Shimabuku Taro, who taught it to me. The *kata* has come to be called *Yara no Kusanku* (Kyan's interpretation of the *Kusanku kata*) and it is the highly regarded last *kata* of the Matsubayashi school.

KARATE ENLIGHTENMENT

Continuing on with Master Kyan, I would like to introduce an episode about Sensei when he had to lower himself to hauling a cart. At that time there was a huge man named Matsuda who had a rough reputation with young villagers. One day Kyan Sensei scolded Matsuda about his rough behavior. Matsuda responded by telling Kyan that in spite of his great physical talent Kyan knew nothing about real confrontations, as *kata* and actual fighting were completely different. Moreover, Matsuda continued to say, he would be happy to take this opportunity to give Kyan a demonstration of exactly what he meant.

They met on the banks of the Hija River where a crowd of villagers anxiously awaited. In an open space just beside the river, the young villagers gathered with great excitement as Kyan Sensei faced the giant Matsuda. Without delay, Matsuda lunged at the tiny Kyan in an effort to strike him in the solar plexus with his fist. Just at that moment, however, Kyan side-stepped and responded by driving his shin into the sciatic junction of Matsuda's quadriceps, which resulted in his huge body tumbling into the river in tremendous pain. So quickly had the encounter ended that everyone was astonished, including Matsuda himself, who, in spite of his damaged leg, became an instant believer and apparently went on to change his nasty attitude, too.

In spite of his poverty, Kyan Sensei managed to build his own house near the Hijabashi. There, he taught karate to a number of young villagers in his yard. Additionally, Master Kyan also taught karate at the Kadena police station and the College of Agriculture and Forestry, the school where Nakazato Joen, the present head of the Okinawan Karate-do Renmei, first learned under him.

Even to this day I still value and keep Kyan's teachings alive: "First of all you must achieve inner-stability, if you are to ever truly embrace karate throughout your entire life. Find an occupation suitable for your character, and one which will provide you with the opportunity to pursue karate." In my case, I became a policeman.

After gaining employment as a prefectural law enforcement officer, I was transferred to the Kadena police station in December of 1931. I danced for joy because I could be near where Kyan Sensei lived. However, before I was able to actually study under Kyan Sensei himself, I first learned his favorite *kata* (*Passai, Chinto,* and *Kusanku,*) from Arakaki Ankichi and Shimabuku Taro. Because he was so small, Kyan Sensei had always trained much harder than everyone else. He always said that training was "seventy percent perspiration and thirty percent inspiration."

Another example that Kyan Sensei often used to describe the importance of consistency in practice concerned hitting the *makiwara*. "If one trains every day," said Kyan, "one can actually break boards or tiles effortlessly. However, by the same token, if one discontinues one's *makiwara* training, one's fist will lose its conditioning. So too in karate, if one trains hard one will achieve remarkable results. However, if one discontinues one's training, one's ability will wither away. Superior conditioning can only be built on relentless effort. The size of one's body is irrelevant." The words of Master Kyan are still very much alive in the privacy of my mind. Just look at me, I am a perfect example of his wisdom. Although I never had the physique or talent, I always adhered to his advice and trained hard.

During Master Kyan's era, *kakedameshi* (a test of skill and spirit through actual contact grappling/striking)[10] was a popular practice among confident men of karate. Chan Mi-Gwa rarely, if ever, refused any challenge from hot-blooded young men, and never lost a single match. In spite of people in the old days saying that such men of karate did not live long lives, Sensei lived until the ripe old age of seventy-six. His death at seventy-six must certainly be a testimony to the fact that men of the discipline can, and do, live to ripe old ages if and when they take good care of themselves. His technique was equaled only by his passion to improve it.

Unfortunately, Kyan Sensei was born during a rather tumultuous generation and lived his life out in humble poverty under less-than-perfect conditions. Perhaps then, it is in those "less-than-perfect conditions" that we find the circumstances conducive to Master Kyan's penchant for karate.

I would like to introduce another episode about Kyan Sensei's life. Incidentally, this story was passed on to me by the late Mr. Kudaka Kori, a man I knew since childhood. Kudaka Sensei first told me this story in the summer of 1975 when he was back in Okinawa on vacation from his home in Tokyo, where he headed up his Shorinji-ryu *dojo* in Tokyo's Shinjuku district.

In August of 1930, Kyan Sensei, Kuwae Ryosei (the last disciple of Bushi Matsumura), and Kudaka Kori all demonstrated *karate-jutsu* at the *Butokuden* in Taipei. Before the demonstration began a big Japanese named Ishida Shinzou, a judo 6th dan, came to the dressing room to pay them a visit. Ishida was the judo teacher at the Taipei (Japanese occupied) police station. "I want to fight with a *karateka* for the purpose of studying its value" announced Ishida. "I am not interested in trying to kill anyone," he insisted. "Therefore, in the interest of research, please consider my challenge."

Despite being surprised by Ishida's unexpected proposal, the karate masters reasoned that there could very well be a bigger problem if they declined his offer. Then there was also the loss of face that would not go over very well back in Okinawa. It would do nothing to enhance the image of the art if they refused to fight with the judoka. They realized that there was much more at stake than a simple bout between a judoka and karateka; it was a matter of honor.

Deciding to accept the offer, the three needed to choose who would fight Ishida. After a brief discussion, Kyan Sensei decided that he would take on the Japanese judoka simply because Kuwae was too old and Kudaka was too young. Removing his good demonstration *gi,* for fear of damaging it, Sensei stood ever so thin by comparison before Ishida, dressed only in his flimsy underwear.

Kyan relaxed in a natural, but ready, stance, and prepared fully to engage the younger and more powerful opponent. Concentrating on his *ki* energy, Kyan patiently waited for Ishida to move into his combative posture. As Ishida lunged forward to grab Kyan (the way in which a judoka often attacks), Sensei faded back into a *nekoashi dachi* (cat stance). Just as the judoka was about to grasp onto the smaller karateka, Kyan drove his left thumb into the mouth of his attacker. This would have been a dangerous move under normal circumstances, but Kyan knew exactly how to place his thumb, between the outside of the teeth and the inside of the cheek, so that it would not be bitten off. Seizing the outside of the cheek with the other four fingers in an attempt to separate the skin from the bone, Sensei stomped down on his right foot which rendered the judoka off balance and immobile. Pulling him down to the ground by the inside of the cheek, Sensei thrust a good clean hammer fist punch down to the jaw near the mastoid process, stopping it just before making contact. Never having experienced anything quite like that, the terrified Ishida instantly submitted, as defeat was obvious. Following the bout, Kudaka, Kuwae, and Sensei put on a successful demonstration. Ishida, in good spirits, asked for and received daily instruction from Sensei until his return to Okinawa.

Never having heard of this kind of gruesome technique, I wondered how effective it would be if used in an unexpected way. Hence, I tried it with a couple of my students and found that it was really effective, especially when one is being grabbed. Kudaka Sensei also believed that the real reason Sensei stripped down to his underwear was to reduce the possibility of being thrown if the judoka actually was able to grasp onto him. The thin underwear would be an ineffective *gi* simply because it would rip when grabbed with any power.

I don't think that it was an easy task to think up such an effective response under that emergency situation. Nonetheless, Kyan Sensei did it. His knowledge of such things clearly demonstrated his understanding of techniques no longer practiced in modern karate. This kind of technique resulted from the deep study of aggressive human behavior generations ago by spiritual recluses in the monastic sanctuary of Shaolin. Studied, further enhanced, haphazardly reinterpreted, and finally codified into application practice, such principles have all but disappeared in modern karate. It is deeply important that we study the true value of ancient *kata* in an effort to fully understand the magnitude of its actual application. In doing so we can come to know that which became obvious to men like Kyan Chotoku.

I built my own twelve *tsubo* (twenty-four *tatami* mat) *dojo* in Naha's Sogenji district in May of 1942. At that time it was the biggest private school of karate in all of Naha. During the grand opening demonstration, I was deeply honored by the presence of many great guests, including Major General Kanna Kenwa, Matayoshi Kenwa from the Ryukyu Shinpo-sha, Dr. Tomoyori Hidehiko, and many others. However, the greatest guest of them all was Kyan Chotoku Sensei. He came all the way from Yomitan village, with his assistant Arakaki Ansei (the brother of Arakaki Ankichi), and demonstrated both *kata* and the *bo* (six-foot wooden staff). Kyan Sensei was then seventy-three years old. Watching the old master perform filled my eyes with tears because I was so deeply moved by his obvious mastery of *budo*, his determination to support me regardless of the great distance and his age, and his life-long dedication to karate.

Even at his advanced age, the other guests were in awe of not only Kyan's sharp and powerful movements but also the master's indomitable spirit. Sensei really looked great at that time. It was, nonetheless, the last official demonstration of his life. That, for me, was also a very meaningful consideration. Scarcity of food and the widespread destruction of war forced Kyan Sensei to evacuate his home in Yomitan to Ishikawa City. How much the wear and tear of war had on his deteriorating health and mental stability remains unknown, but the great master of karate, Kyan Chotoku, died on September 20, 1945, at the age of seventy-six.

THE MOTTO OF KARATE-DO

Because of his tiny size, Sensei spent considerable time and effort developing his *jodan-tsuki* (ris-

ing punch). Never having altered this technique, Kyan's *jodan-tsuki* represents his own interpretation of using the strike in a practical way for a person of his size. It can be said that his unique *jodan-tsuki* exists in no other *ryuha* and must therefore illustrate his own understanding of karate-do. For a man of his size, Sensei knew his strengths and weaknesses well. His personal motto was that "effort is everything." In many ways, so too was my training motto based on Master Kyan's original-ity and ideas. It is as follows:

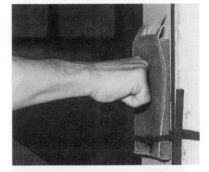

The basic way of hitting a *makiwara*.

Kyan's original punch.

1. We are all children of God.
2. The boundaries of human achievement lie only in the mind.
3. Seek to always improve the intensity of your training.
4. If he practices five times, I'll do it seven times or ten times.
5. Never depend on others. Miyamoto Musashi said "Respect the gods and Buddha too, but never depend on them."
6. Believe in yourself, and embrace the *shingitai* principles.
7. Karate teaches that the real enemy lies within. Get interested in the pursuit not just the possession, the race not just the goal. Effort is everything.

8. Learn to live in harmony with nature and your fellow man, rather than frivolously trying to destroy it or dominate them. Travel the middle path.

HIGHLIGHTS OF THREE CLASSICAL KATA

Bringing this chapter to an end, I would like to illustrate some of the principal techniques from the classical *kata Passai, Chinto,* and *Kusanku.* Although these *kata* are practiced by many different schools, the way I teach them is exactly the way that Kyan Sensei handed them down to Arakaki Ankichi and Shimabuku Taro.

PASSAI

It is said that *Passai* was created by an unknown master long ago. Yet, in spite of the origins of this *kata* being lost in the sands of time, *Passai* remains one the principal *kata* of karate-do, and is now regarded as *koryu* (ancient stream) *kata.* Handed down in and around the district of Tomari, *Passai* was one of Kyan Sensei's favorite forms until the day he died.

Sokuto-geri, foot-edge kick.

Suiraken no kamae, drunkard fighting posture.

Sagurite no kamae, searching-hand fighting posture.

Chinto is another ancient *kata* whose origins, like *Passai,* have been lost to karate history. Once the favorite kata of Arakaki Ankichi, it was a popular practice handed down in and around the district of Tomari, and remains a principal *kata* of *koryu.*

Heisoku-dachi, standing kamae

Magetori-barai-uke, both knife-hands are swept away above the forehead to remove the hands of the opponent who is holding you by the hair.

Kyobu-soete shuto-uchi, chest augmented knife-hand strike.

It is believed that this unique kata represents the defensive principles once taught by a Chinese martial artist named Kusanku, who visited Okinawa. Proof of his existence can be located in the 1761 publication titled *Oshima Hikki*. The favorite *kata* of Kyan Sensei, it was taught to him by Chatan Yara *Peichin*.

Soto-hachiji shizentai-dachi, **natural posture.**

Ryu-no-shita no kamae, **dragon-tongue fighting posture.**

Ura-gamae, **cheating fighting posture.**

Chapter 9

MOTOBU CHOKI SENSEI:
THE MASTER FIGHTER

MOTOBU "THE MONKEY"

Motobu Choki was born in February of 1871 in Shuri's Akahira village. He was the third son of Motobu Chomo Udon, and from a family of position in the old Ryukyu Kingdom. As was the case for all firstborn males, Choyu, Motobu's older brother, received a proper education in the Confucian *classics* and Japanese language. Naturally, he was also well schooled in the martial art traditions befitting the son of a *kemochi*. However, as was the rule during that era, the second and subsequent children did not usu-

Motobu Choki

ally receive equal attention. Such was the case with Motobu Choki.

It is believed that Motobu Choki resented his upbringing and developed a fierce temper in childhood. Whatever the case, he grew up without a proper education and was lacking academic ambition. However, he did fancy himself physically talented and longed to one day be the strongest man in all of Okinawa.

Like many athletes who lack formal training in their endeavor, aptitude and determination make up for a lot, and Motobu had enough of both. Without formal instruction, Motobu Choki virtually trained himself. He relentlessly struck the *makiwara* and trained daily with *chishi* until his body grew exceptionally strong. In spite of not learning any particular style of karate, he ultimately became known as "Motobu no Saru" (Motobu the Monkey), because of his penchant for martial arts, great strength, and uncanny ability to swing in a tree. Motobu Choki's training was without question fanatical, and his ability clearly indicated the merits of such a regimen.

Motobu often cruised the *Tsuji* (red-light) district of Naha at night after the theaters closed. While never actually initiating a fight, one could say that Motobu Saru never walked away from one, either. In fact, he took pride in frequently challenging anyone on the busy street who caused trouble. In the *Tsuji*, late at night, there never seemed to be a shortage of men with aggressive attitudes. Hence, Motobu Choki often tested his skill and spirit through the ever-popular *kakedameshi*.

One night a challenge brought Motobu into contact with a man named Itarashiki. Itarashiki, who was older than Motobu by five or six years, was famous for his *kakedameshi,* and easily defeated the cocky Motobu. Motobu could not sleep the night he was defeated, reassessing his opponent's technique and strategy over and over. From that time forth, Motobu devoted himself to karate with an intensity he had not previously known.

His single-minded passion to be one of the strongest men in Okinawa, coupled with his violent behavior, was, as one might imagine, frowned on by any intelligent teacher. Motobu Saru, like most other hot-blooded young men, was unable to understand why no one wanted to teach him. The only master who would provide any instruction for young Motobu was Matsumora Kosaku Chikudon Peichin in Tomari. And that, so they say, resulted only because Motobu was relentless in his pursuit to learn from him. He went to Matsumora virtually every day asking for instruction, which ultimately resulted in his being taught both the *Naihanchi* and *Passai kata.*

It was Motobu's acquaintance, the popular Okinawan musician named Kin Ryojin (1873–1936), who acted as the intermediary for Motobu Saru's first meeting with Matsumora Sensei. During his intense study of Ryukyuan music, Mr. Kin, like other people of wealth and position, often enjoyed lessons in karate from Master Matsumora, in an effort to maintain good health and keep himself occupied with activities other than just music. Living not too far from Tomari, Kin always travelled from Shuri to see the great master by horse and took Motobu with him. Motobu often asked if Matsumora would practice *tegumi* (application training) with him. However, Matsumora always refused because he knew that Motobu would use his newfound technique over in the *Tsuji* that evening. Rather, Matsumora Sensei told

Motobu, "Don't be so concerned about sparring with me, or others, for that matter. You will find what works best for you, but only after you have discovered the real adversary—the enemy within." Notwithstanding, Motobu Saru secretly observed Matsumora's *tegumi* lessons with other disciples from behind the courtyard wall during special training in the evenings.

I would like to impart a rather heartwarming episode of Motobu's tenacity, which was originally told to me by Kin Ryojin. There once was a huge commoner named Komesu Magii from the Gaja district in Nishibaru village. At the time, he was reputed to be the strongest wrestler in all of Okinawa. In recounting the incident, it was said that Komesu is even much bigger than the enormous judo 6th dan named Yamashiro, who was a teacher at the prefectural second junior school. In 1888, when Motobu Sensei was about seventeen or eighteen years old, he happened to meet Komesu Magii quite by accident. Naturally, meeting the biggest and strongest wrestler in Okinawa meant—if you were Motobu Choki—an opportunity to test your skill and pick up a few pointers. Hence, Motobu petitioned Komesu to a bout.

Interested in learning more about Komesu, I visited Nagamine Shoshu at his residence in Shuri's Kinjo-cho on the 19th of February of 1979. Although familiar with both Ryukyu history and martial arts, Komesu Magii gained much of his strength and technique working on the Yanbaru ships transporting firewood. When Komesu retired at thirty years old, he was undefeated in wrestling. After looking into the history of Komesu, I discovered that he died in 1918 at the age of sixty-four, which would have made him fifteen or sixteen years older than Motobu Sensei.

Recognizing the potential danger in injuring the son of a nobleman, Komesu Magii politely refused, saying that "it was improper for commoners to engage important people of position. I'm just a peasant and you shouldn't tease me so." Motobu Sensei responded by telling Komesu that while he admired his concern, it was not him he was so interested in fighting, but rather the opportunity to discover and analyze the differences between karate and wrestling. With that explanation Motobu concluded by asking that Komesu reconsider his request and accept a friendly bout with him. Komesu Magii gladly accepted.

As Motobu did not have a proper *obi* (belt) needed for such grappling bouts, he made do with a makeshift straw rope from a shed in the yard where they faced each other. Komesu told the young *kemochi* to grip onto his obi in any way he wanted. Sensei tried to hold onto Komesu's *obi* as best he could but his opponent was just too big and powerful for the much smaller Motobu. Yet, and in the midst of certain defeat, Sensei remained confident because

The kata of Okinawan sumo.

he thought that he would be able to force his well-trained iron fists into the various vital points in and around his opponent's waist. Finally, and only after Sensei tried his best, Motobu shouted out in defeat.

During that time, men still wore their hair in the topknot style. Sensei asked Komesu if one's topknot was grabbed from behind what could one do?

Magii politely responded by fiercely grabbing Motobu's topknot from behind. Struggling vigorously, Motobu was unable to gain his stability, being rendered completely helpless against the great power of Komesu. The wrestling bout and topknot experience with Komesu proved to Motobu that, regardless of one's physical prowess in karate, it was not always possible to overcome someone whose size and power were so dissimilar.

In his later years Motobu told me that "the applications of *kata* have their limits and one must come to understand this. The techniques of *kata* were never developed to be used against a professional fighter, in an arena or on the battlefield. They were, however, most effective against someone who had no idea of the strategy being used to counter their aggressive behavior." Motobu continued to say that "a small man must improve his technique as much as he can, and discover how it can be used regardless of time, place, and opponent. In spite of a street encounter never being the same, the principles of the *kata* never vary, however. Thus, one must learn how they are applied and how to bend with the winds of adversity." Motobu recited an interesting poem which has been handed down in karate history.

Poem:

> *Kataya Kataadami Wajiya wajiyasadami*
> *Hindeiwajiyashiranu Nuyakutachuga*

Interpretation:

> *Kata* and *waza* (technique) are both limited by themselves.
> They are useless until one learns how to apply
> them in any situation

I would like to introduce a story which brought a lot of attention to karate on Japan's mainland, and won popularity for Motobu Sensei all over the country. It was in early 1921 that Motobu Sensei left Okinawa and ventured to Osaka, where he became employed as a guard for a large company. One weekend he and a friend took a short journey to nearby Kyoto where a fighting competition "open to all" was being held at the *Butokuden*. While observing the opening bouts Motobu carefully analyzed each performance, pondering how he would have handled each situation. All of a sudden a big foreigner, about six feet tall, entered the ring, shouting out in a language no one could understand. Completely baffled, Motobu Sensei wondered what the foreigner was doing, when the ring announcer, appearing in the middle of the ring, said "Ladies and Gentleman, if you are confident, we have a prize for anyone who will test their power and strength against the foreigner."

The special attraction of the day, some say it was the way in which the foreigner paraded around the ring showing off, leering out at the audience, and challenging the audience with exaggerated gestures, that finally provoked Motobu. Whatever the case, nobody accepted the challenge and the foreigner became even more arrogant.

Knowing that Motobu could teach that big foreigner a lesson, Motobu's friend quickly ran up to the ring announcer and told him that he had someone to accept the challenge. When the ring announcer told the audience that there was someone to accept the foreigner's challenge, a great applause filled the hall. Motobu quickly made ready to engage the foreigner and entered the ring, where he stood facing his opponent. The foreigner looked uncertain about the unfamiliar posture Motobu assumed. So much smaller than the enormous foreigner was Motobu that it appeared to the audience that he would certainly be defeated.

Underestimating Motobu, the huge foreigner began to provoke him by waving his long arms around as he entered into engagement distance. Ignoring the foreigner's catcalls and insults, Motobu concentrated instead on his distance and strategy. After two rounds, with great speed and an intense *kiai*, Motobu dropped the belligerent foreigner to the canvas, whereupon the bout came to an end. So quickly did Motobu defeat his opponent that the audience was confused, not understanding what had happened.

With Motobu standing calmly over the fallen opponent in the middle of the ring, a hush fell over the audience as they stared in disbelief. The question that immediately spread throughout the audience was "How did Motobu knock out the giant?" Many people suggested that he must have used this or that technique, one person even yelled out "Was that *yawara?*" Actually, it was Motobu's quick strike to his opponent's temple that left the huge foreigner a pile of motionless flesh on the canvas. As the opponent came barging in, Motobu simply side-stepped and caught him in the temple with a short blow from his iron fist. With no one actually having seen karate before, and it happening so fast, no one really knew what happened.

That bout occurred in 1921 when Motobu was fifty-two or fifty-three years old. It became quite a popular topic of discussion throughout the entire nation, especially among martial artists. Like any popular event, however, so too was Motobu's fight subject to misinterpretation when recounted by some.

I feel certain that I got the details correct because it was Motobu Sensei who told me directly. Demonstrating his strength and taking on all comers, the foreigner in question was presumed to be a well-known professional prizefighter who was travelling around the Orient under the pretense of being a white Russian named John Kentelu. However, there seems to be a question about his credentials and even his name.

At any rate, Motobu Saru became quite a popular figure after defeating that foreigner, and *King* magazine went on to feature the proverbial "David vs. Goliath" bout in a special article in 1925. Recounting the incident, the story made for great reading and helped promote the effectiveness of karate on the mainland of Japan. Having gained enormous notoriety, Motobu Sensei was the first to start teaching karate (then still called Ryukyu *kempo to-te jutsu*) in the Kansai district, and also in Tokyo's Hongo Dai-machi. As karate became a popular practice Motobu began teaching at local universities in Tokyo and elsewhere.

When one looks back on those early days, there can be no question that Motobu Choki's efforts to promote karate provided ample grounds to conclude that the discipline was, at the very least, both a practical and effective tool for self-defense. His younger contemporary, Funakoshi Gichin, in spite of their personal differences, was a man who sought to cultivate karate as an art form, and is recognized as such. As different as day and night, their collective impact on the growth and direction of karate remains, even to this day, an important lesson in understanding the magnitude of this profound tradition.

These photos of Motobu were taken around 1931, when Sensei moved up from Osaka to open his dojo in Tokyo's Hongo district. He was about sixty years old at the time.

The opponent is attacking with a left punch to the face. Sensei steps in with his left foot, and, at the same time blocks the attack and counters with an ura-ken to the opponent's face, while continuing to protect his own stomach with the blocking hand.

This photo shows what to do when caught from behind. The body moves down and out to the side as one arm blocks while the other elbow strikes the opponent's solar plexus.

The opponent's right arm is around the neck and his left hand is holding the right arm. At the moment he tries to control you, strike the neck with the left hand and prevent his action.

The opponent punches with a right chudan-tsuki. As he punches, close the distance by stepping in with the left foot and counter him effectively, taking the opponent's joint with the left hand, while stopping him, yet protecting your own vital points at the same time with the right hand.

Having stopped the opponent's punches and grabbed his arms, sensei kicks him in the groin.

The opponent attacks with a right punch to the face. Sensei will then catch the right arm and grab the opponent's testicles.

THE ENORMOUS POWER OF THE KEIKOKEN

In April of 1936, I, as a police officer, was sent to Tokyo to study at the Metropolitan Police Department for six months. It was during that time that I received lessons from Master Motobu Choki at his *dojo* in Hongo Dai-machi. I remember during that time Sensei often saying how very happy he was that karate had become such a popular practice in and around Tokyo. However, I also remember his melancholy. He was sad that with the popularity of the discipline there also came great change. The *kata* practiced in Tokyo had been carelessly changed, and in some cases had completely disintegrated. In Okinawa during the old days students spent years meticulously learning a single *kata* or two. That custom in Tokyo had changed to the pointless but popular practice of accumulating many *kata* without ever understanding their respective applications. The practice of *kata* had been reduced to stiff and fixed postures, without *tai sabaki* (body movement) or *ashi sabaki* (stepping and sliding.) *Kata* had become a lifeless practice, Motobu believed. He also said that when I returned to Okinawa, I should petition men like his *senpai*, Yabu Kentsu, to study orthodox *koryu kata* and one day bring it back to Tokyo.

In spite of Master Motobu having started karate on his own, he ultimately came to recognize the limits of practicing that way and sought out the formal instruction of Matsumora Kosaku. After developing his technique to an unquestionably high standard, and mastering the *kata,* Motobu Sensei reinterpreted the common principles on which the discipline rested and, in doing so, established an innovative way of teaching karate. Regardless of the gossip, Master Motobu had enormous respect for orthodox *kata* and knew that, in spite of actual street encounters never being the same, the principles of the *kata* never changed. While I was learning under Motobu Sensei, we always took the study of *kata* very seriously, and spent much time practicing its application and movement.

Through no shortage of practical experience Master Motobu had developed considerable confidence in the application of his technique. Motobu Choki created such a synthesis with his karate that his life became as much a product of the art, as the art had become a product of his life. Compared to the fighting traditions which had been handed down in and around the districts of Shuri and Tomari, Motobu carried the position of his hands relatively high when blocking and striking. Indicative of southern Chinese boxing, he also chambered his fists quite high around the level of the nipple beside the lungs for better defense and attitude, he said. As I had previously mentioned, one of the master's favorite techniques was his *keikoken-zuki* (forefinger-knuckle punch), developed through intensive *makiwara* training, a practice which he had strictly adhered to from childhood. Many people I

The *keiko* fist was favored by Motobu.

have seen have struck the *makiwara* since that time, but never have I seen anyone reproduce the awesome power generated by Master Motobu. His *keikoken* was, pardon the play on words, truly shocking.

Sensei often expounded on the importance of understanding *maai* (engagement distance) and *ma* (the space or interval created by *taisabaki*) in an effort to effectively use one's techniques. "Not being able to place oneself in a position superior to the opponent would," Sensei said, "unquestionably make any subsequent technique virtually ineffective. The utmost attention must be placed on learning to position oneself correctly, and make the best use of the space or interval created by moving one's body in an effort to effectively subjugate any opponent."

It is wholly due to those lessons from Sensei that I actually went on to devise the seven *yakusoku kumite kata* based on my understanding of Shorin-ryu karate. In an effort to better explain, let me elaborate from the teachings of Motobu Choki. Master Motobu said: "When you face an opponent be sure to assume a posture which is not too wide. A posture which is too wide is impractical and leaves one with little mobility. Mobility is the foundation of responding effectively. One must move freely, instinctively, and intelligently. Body language is important; never telegraph your intentions. Liberate yourself from fixed postures and seek to cultivate unconstrained technique and movement."

During the six months that I trained under Master Motobu in Tokyo, his teachings were so provocative that I constantly pondered the value of his advice. In an effort to gain an even deeper understanding of his lessons, I meticulously analyzed the tactics of Miyamoto Musashi, along with the strategy of other warriors too, by reading many books on the art of the sword. When I had completed my study of his lessons I formed hypotheses and presented them to Master Motobu, which he approved. I will list them in order:

1. The ideal technique, whether it be hand or foot, is one which can provide an effective simultaneous defense and offense.
2. One should strive to use both hands simultaneously in a defensive and offensive manner.
3. The hands and feet must be used in conjunction with each other to maximize optimal defensive and offensive performance.
4. Seek to understand the value of angular movement. Never face an opponent directly, and learn body change through mastering foot movement.
5. If you catch the opponent's kick retaliate in kind. If he catches your kick then quickly kick him with the other foot. You must always think about taking the initiative.

The above five items must not only be understood theoretically; one must diligently train in an effort to be able to apply them instinctively. In retrospect, even after more than fifty years of studying karate-do, I still can't help but admire Motobu Sensei, and feel truly fortunate to have had the opportunity to learn under a man of such skill and insight.

As Sensei desired, he finally returned to Okinawa in the autumn of 1936. There he visited many of his colleagues to describe the situation of karate-do on the mainland. He also spent considerable time and effort researching ancient *kata* and *kobudo* before returning to Tokyo. He returned to Okinawa again in the spring of 1939, where he remained until his death in August of 1944.

Peacefully departing this world at the age of seventy-four, Master Motobu passed away in the home which I rented for him in Naha's Sogenji district. I am grateful to have become so close to the Master in his later years. It was a time when he imparted many valuable things to me, including his favorite techniques. It was also my pleasure to have discovered many of his ideas about, what he described as, "living karate," which had a profound impact on the way in which I came to embrace the discipline. I learned much from Master Motobu Choki. He lived his life with a zest for karate like no one I ever knew, and, even to this day, I still feel the impact which that remarkable man had on me, and of my understanding of this humble tradition.

Chapter 10

ARAKAKI ANKICHI:
THE YOUNG AND MULTI-TALENTED
BUSHI

TOE KICKER EXTRAORDINAIRE

Born in Shuri's Akata village in November of 1899, Arakaki Ankichi was the first of eleven children. After becoming wealthy liquor merchants, his family relocated to Tori-hori village. Ankichi was a quiet, but intelligent, boy during primary school and led his class in academic achievement. However, by the time he entered junior high school he became absorbed in athletics and gradually began to ignore his studies, until he finally dropped out all together in the ninth grade.

Arakaki Ankichi

As a youth he started taking karate from his primary school teacher, Gusukuma Shinpan, and later from Hanashiro Chomo, who was his teacher in junior high school.

After dropping out of school he intensified his training in karate under Chibana Choshin, a young master who, like Arakaki, lived in the town. Of normal height and weight, Arakaki was put together like an Olympic athlete, possessed great coordination, and was naturally talented.

Being the first son of a rather wealthy family, Arakaki was able to pursue his passion with the complete support of his parents. This resulted in the development of an incredible talent. In just a few short years of diligent study under the direction of Chibana, Arakaki became renowned as "Uwayaguwa Ankichi" (Ankichi of Uwayaguwa), a name which associated him to his family's liquor shop in Tori-hori.[11]

At age nineteen, Ankichi took part in the annual Okinawa *sumo* wrestling tournament at Shuri's Memorial Field. During the tournament he came finally to face an enormous opponent named Kamiya from Yomitan village. The audience was sure that Kamiya would certainly defeat the much smaller Arakaki with sheer size alone. However, so supple and strong were Arakaki's legs that he managed to outmaneuver the bigger opponent and walk away the victor. The audience was astonished to have seen such unexpected technique, and I can only can imagine just how impressive he must have been during that time. Many said that Arakaki Ankichi was in the same class as famous *yokozuna* (grand champions) like Sakumoto Nabe and Yabe Kenshin.

In spite of his inborn talent and remarkable coordination, Arakaki Sensei was more known for his piercing *tsumasaki-geri* (toe-kick) than as a master of karate. This kick was enthusiastically described as penetrating!

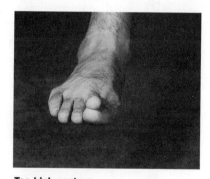

Toe kick posture.

In junior high school Arakaki practiced such sports as judo, wrestling, and swimming. Besides partaking in sports because he liked them, the young Arakaki specifically wanted to train his powerful legs. He was so intent on becoming strong that he continued his sports conditioning program morning, noon, and night. Additionally, he also climbed trees, relentlessly practiced various jumping kicks, and often walked up to Bengadake, the mountain district of Shuri, on his toes! Continuing his cross training for an entire year, Arakaki ultimately forged a well-conditioned body quite capable of responding effectively in a self-defense situation, and, of course, toes of steel!

Once, when Sensei was around twenty years old, he and some of his friends were in a tea house in *Tsuji* drinking and having a good time. While getting up to go to the toilet, he accidentally bumped into a big man who insisted on picking a quarrel with him in the corridor on the second floor. Trying to ignore the man, Sensei was unable to get out of his way, which resulted in Sensei being shoved down the staircase. Being in such good physical condition, Arakaki was able to

Gusukuma Shinpan

roll down the stairs avoiding injury. The enraged man leaped down ·the stairs and grabbed Arakaki by the arm, trying to yank him up in an effort to punch his face. Seizing the man's arm with the other hand, Sensei drove his toes deeply into the armpit of his attacker, which resulted in the man dropping to the ground unconscious.

Needless to say, Sensei never returned to that tea house again. About six months later, while reading the newspaper one morning, Ankichi was shocked to see a story which described some big wrestler who had died as a result of injuries sustained by "some karate expert" at a tea house in *Tsuji*. The article went on to say that "survived by two daughters, both of whom were serious judoka, the family sought to revenge the death of their beloved father." In spite of the man allegedly dying sometime after his encounter with Arakaki, the police were never

called in, and a subsequent investigation was unable to provide the actual reason for his death.

Another time, Ansuke, Arakaki's younger brother, who disliked martial arts of any kind, challenged Ankichi to kick him, recklessly believing that he would not be injured. Making fun of his older brother, Ansuke said "I'll let you kick my body if you give me ten yen." In those days even one yen would have been enough to let you drink and stay overnight in the red-light district of *Tsuji*. Pressed for

Hanashiro Chomo

money, Ansuke reasoned that he could easily handle his brother's kick and then go on a spending spree with the ten yen!

Accepting his offer, Arakaki launched his awesome toe kick directly into the right thigh of his brother. Although Arakaki's kick

106

was not full powered it left his poor brother in terrible pain. In a couple of days the bruise festered up with a fever and Ansuke had to go into the hospital to have an operation on the area where he was hit.

At the time I had interviewed him, Ansuke was about eighty years old and lived in comfort composing *haiku* poems. In spite of Ansuke's age, his thigh still clearly carried the scar of Ankichi's kick. Visiting Arakaki's home with my colleague Higa Yuchoku, my mind was filled with the warm memory of Arakaki Sensei and I couldn't help but feel a little sad not having seen my teacher for so many years.

Another fascinating story about Arakaki Ankichi was told to me by Oyama Chojo, the former mayor of Koza-city, in April of 1968 at the opening of the new Onoyama swimming pool. It was around 1920 when Sensei passed his physical examination for the military draft. Because he was in such remarkable physical condition, he was put into the third regiment of the Konoe Division, a unit which consisted only of men with superior physiques.

By the time Oyama enlisted, Arakaki had already been there for approximately two years. Their unit was well known for its dexterity and often made the dangerous river crossing at Tone, a body of water known for having the strongest current in Japan. Once they had to swim for two kilometers to reach the boat before returning to their starting point. Many men needed assistance, some were even unable to finish the 4km swim, but it was Arakaki who arrived first. Well liked by everyone, Arakaki was praised for his dauntless attitude, which was second only to his kind personality and moral character.

Kyan Chotoku

Around 1921, after Arakaki was honorably discharged from the military, he went to live in the Kadena district of Chatan village, where his family ran a thriving branch of their liquor store. It was during that time that Arakaki met and began his training with Master Kyan. Kyan Sensei lived by the Hija bridge in Yomitan, the village next to Kadena, where Arakaki had relocated. Arakaki was about twenty-five years old when he began to study under the fifty-five-year-old Kyan. It was a perfect time for the mellow teacher and young student to be brought together. Master Kyan taught diligently and Arakaki put everything he had into learning karate under his taskmaster.

A PROFOUND KNOWLEDGE OF MUSIC, FOLK DANCE, AND CLASSICAL DRAMA

When I was twenty years old, I first studied under Arakaki Sensei through an introduction from my *senpai*, Shimabuku Taro. Arakaki Sensei was then twenty-eight years old. His modern approach to teaching karate with scientific explanations, the quoting of historical facts, and stories of martial arts in general, fascinated me right away. I learned karate under him for one year until I was called for military service. I was sent to Kyushu where I served in Ooita Prefecture with the infantry for eighteen months before returning to Okinawa to again train with Arakaki Sensei. In spite of the great length of time which has passed since that time I still clearly recall his three theses:

1. "Cultivated in Okinawa, karate-do has an enormous legacy. If you want to dedicate your life to karate-do, you must first establish financial security."
2. "Living in accordance with the principles of karate-do also means forging enough inner strength so that you never regret your decision for having done so." Arakaki Sensei said that people who look down on, or ridicule, our local culture as being somewhat backward by nature, obviously have inferiority complexes. Regardless of such shortcomings, such people have called our local (folk) musicians *utaguwaa narayun,* or people who waste their time studying unimportant music; calligraphers have been labeled *jiiguwaa narayun,* or people who waste their time studying unimportant writing; and, karateka have been designated *teiiguwaa narayun,* or people who waste their time studying karate. Hence, it is with this in mind that I believe one needs to establish more than just a physical mastery of karate-do. If one is to understand, and bear this common prejudice, an inner fortitude becomes a necessary prerequisite
3. "There are similarities between karate and the fine arts. For example, in the case of dancing, the principles of movement are quite comparable; the oscillation of the limbs, use of the body, breathing, centering, and the use of the *tanden* (spot in the abdomen). Yet, in spite of dance and martial arts sharing corresponding similarities, they are not the same. Karate is a discipline which surfaced from man's instinctive efforts to defend himself. As the discipline continued to grow it came to address the issues surrounding life and death. As karate ultimately unfolded as an art form it provided a spiritual path on which

its followers could discover and conquer the sources of human weakness."

In 1920, the Shuri Fire Fund Association sponsored a classical art and dance performance at Shuri castle's *Kita-no-Udon* (then the Shuri public hall). In one part of the program titled *A Child of Morikawa*, Arakaki Sensei performed the monkey *kumi-odori* (monkey folk-dance). Because of his incredible strength and skills, Arakaki was truly able to bring his performance to life. As he performed, he jumped up onto the big column of the stage and then climbed it upside down. He rolled sideways and mimicked a monkey

The author performs *Karate-Do Sanka.* Jikoen Temple, Honolulu, Hawaii. December 15, 1996. *Photo by Wayne Muromoto*

perfectly. He even picked a lit cigarette out from the mouth of a man in the audience with his toes and puffed on it. His striking performance, in perfect harmony with the music, astonished everyone so much that it became the favorite of the era.

Kita no Udon

Arakaki Sensei also had a profound knowledge of *ryuka* (original Ryukyu poetry). When he was twenty-three years old the Nomura sect of *ryuka* held a ceremony to commemorate the death of its founder, Master Takaesu. The ceremony was held in front of his grave site in the Nakagami district of Chatan Village. Following the five phrase poem recited by the students of the Nomura school, the chairman asked if there was anyone who might like to recite an impromptu poem in honor of the late master. The only person to reply was Arakaki Ankichi, who stood up and recited the following:

Poem:

Kita no Udon
Uteichichamigusoni uzumigoeneran
Narisuminodeishino utaguichichin

Interpretation:

> Even if he could hear the poems recited by
> those familiar to him, our master is unable
> to come back to us. Therefore, it is certain
> that he has found his place of peace now.

Following his recital, Arakaki played the *samisen* (three string guitar) and sang "*San'yama-Bushi*," for which he received unprecedented applause by all the *senpai* present. This story was imparted to me by a late master of *Nomura-ryu* named Kochi Kamechiyo, who was also a respected friend of Arakaki Sensei.

Whenever Arakaki partied in Naha's *Tsuji* district he always vividly displayed his talent for entertaining people. Once he made an entire set of *hyaku nin isshu* (a game which uses 100 cards to illustrate a hundred different kinds of *waka* poems) by using just the empty cigarette packages of the tobacco brand named Golden Bats. Choosing a hundred of his favorite poems by renowned masters, Arakaki skillfully brushed them on the back of as many empty cigarette packages. By doing so he clearly demonstrated not only his knowledge of poetry, but also his skill as a master calligrapher.

Sensei once told me that many martial artists rarely, if ever, cultivate anything beyond their physical skills, and by so doing remain forever unbalanced. "Sadly enough," he said, "they often become gluttons and/or drunks. Embracing martial arts means cultivating alternative pursuits as well. This refers to establishing a balance between the physical and the mental. Cultivating such pursuits prevents one from becoming a drunkard and helps develop a fertile personality." I still remember an interesting poem about drinking that Sensei taught me in those days.

Poem:

> *Kukurushichi numibashiwagotonwashite*
> *sakeya nuchinuburukusuiyashiga*

Interpretation:

> It is best to drink with care, by doing so
> one can not only forget his anxiety, so too
> can he add years to his life.

Two other poems which I can distinctly remember as being among the very favorites of Arakaki Sensei are as follows.

Poem:
> *Namayunakatomibahijashinsasusa*
> *Ahyangarechun urazagumai*

Interpretation:
> Although it still seems to be midnight
> the crack of dawn begins a new day now.
> It looks as if I am destined
> to sleep here again.

POWERFUL ENOUGH TO SEIZE THE FIRST BOLT OF LIGHTNING

Arakaki Sensei encouraged me to learn Ryukyu dance directly under the prominent Master Misato Ansei during my youth, which has had a profound effect on my life. During the time that I was studying under Master Misato he imparted an interesting story to me about Arakaki Sensei:

"Arakaki visited me in *Tsuji's* Hiigurumaa district," recounted Misato, "to ask if I would teach him a dance called *shudon* for the water-pot festival on August 15th. As there were only three days left before the festival I thought it would be virtually impossible to transmit such a difficult tradition, much less have him perform it in front of an audience. Arakaki under-stood my concern but insisted that I teach him regardless of the time factor. I agreed. Together, we borrowed a room in the red-light district and I taught him throughout the entire night. Much to my surprise, Arakaki mastered all the steps in about five hours or so. The following day we reviewed the dance sever-al times before he hurried back home to practice. I bumped into Arakaki some time after the local festival and he expressed his grat-itude for my instruction. Even though it was just a local village

The author performs *Kanuyo Bushi*. Jikoen Temple, Honolulu, Hawaii. December 15, 1996. *Photo by Wayne Muromoto*

festival Arakaki worked as if it was a professional exhibition and mastered an incredibly difficult tradition in a few days. Not only was I deeply impressed by his commitment, but also by his diligence and skill. From that time forward I was filled with admiration for Arakaki Ankichi."

Having established such popularity during that time allowed Arakaki to become politically involved with the growth and direction of dance and theater in and around Kadena village. His chief rival was a man named Onaha Zenko. Onaha was a strong leader in the eastern part of the village, while Arakaki controlled the western suburb. They became friendly rivals, if there is such a thing, and went on to compete for power in such districts as Mijigama, Kaneku, Noguni, Chatan, and Yara. Even to this day the Ryukyu arts are still popular in and around the Chatan and Kadena districts.

The ink drawing and poem illustrated by Arakaki is similar to the poem written about Higaonna Kanryo and reads: *"Kuken karate hatsukaminario toriosafu"* ("Powerful enough to seize the first bolt of lightning, there's nothing as fierce as the grasp of karate's empty hands"). Illustrating a goblin atop a mountain holding a drum, he signed it *Ichisennin,* "The Hermit." At the request of Dr. Iha Magobe, a man who owned the hospital in Chatan's Yara village, Arakaki Sensei painted the illustration and composed the poem while at a party near Murochi when he was thirty years old. The painting was given to me in January of 1984 by Angi, the brother of Arakaki, who told me that I should keep this in memory of Sensei. I accepted the old painting with deep emotion.

An ink drawing by Arakaki Ankichi.

Coming from a fairly well-to-do family, Arakaki was able to pursue both *budo* and the arts in a way that normal people could not. However, after WW I his father died and the business went into a slump with the recession. Regardless of the effort Arakaki put forth, the business never regained its stature and ultimately went bankrupt. The stress eventually took its toll and Sensei became sick and was never to recover. He passed away at the young age of thirty-one, on December 28, 1929, from stomach ulcers.

While some people are talented and specialize in only one area, Arakaki Sensei went on to become skilled in many areas, such as karate, sports, Ryukyu music, dance, poetry, and calligraphy. For one so young Arakaki Sensei was both well cultured and adept. He was not only a man of character devoted to karate-do, he was also unique as a *bujin,* a man who placed enormous value on balancing his physical training with artistic study.

Much time has passed since Sensei died but I will never forget my debt of gratitude to him. There is not a year which goes by that I don't pay tribute to the memory of that great man during the anniversary of his death. The modern approach to teaching karate-do that Arakaki Ankichi propagated continues, even to this day, to sink deeper and deeper into my mind. He was a man who had a profound impact on the way I came to embrace both karate and life.

PART TWO

MY PHILOSOPHY OF KARATE-DO

Chapter 11

THE POWER OF MYTH

When considering the value of karate history, and the heroic deeds of those who have walked before us, young people today often complain about not being able to distinguish between fact and fiction. For example, as mentioned earlier, there are far too many tales about such superhuman feats as crossing a ceiling with just the fingers; wrenching off the thigh muscle of a living bull with a *shuto;* small men weighing around a hundred and ten pounds kicking up a sugar barrel far heavier than their own body weight; or crushing bamboo stalks with one's grip!

To see the value in such stories is to understand that Okinawan people have long enjoyed embellishing historical events which serve to teach young people important lessons about life in general. In this way the stories are much more fun to listen to and can be better perpetuated over the generations. Often people ponder the credibility of such feats or imagine how such a master must have trained to accomplish them. In general, these stories are positive and serve to teach important lessons. However, in our world of movies, materialism, and the internet, students often find such stories absurd. It is in this vein that I would like to introduce an example of one person who was truly powerful, so that students might ponder the potential of human power. The man was Nakamura Shoei.

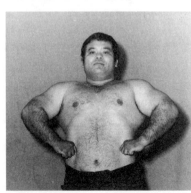

Nakamura Shoei

Nakamura Shoei was born in January of 1945 in Nakazato village on Kume Island near Okinawa. In his forties he was

5 feet 7 inches tall and weighed 258 pounds, with a chest measurement of 54 inches, and a reach of 20 inches. He was a policeman by profession, a 4th dan in judo, and had won twenty-one Okinawan sumo tournaments. Nakamura started power-lifting seriously when he was twenty-four years old and by the time he was twenty-seven he had captured the All Kyushu Power Lifting Championships (lifting 665 kg in total). The following year, at the age of twenty-eight, he went on to win the All Japan Championship (lifting 700 kg in total), a title he held for four consecutive years. In May of 1979, he became a representative for Japan in international competition and finished third in the heavyweight division, bringing great honor to his country and to all Okinawans. Presently, Nakamura's new Japanese record for the squat is 335kg. Put simply, he is a Hercules.

However, power-lifting is not the same as weight-lifting as the techniques and objectives are different. When researching the way old masters used to train with the *chikarasaashi* (old stone bar bells once used in Fuzhou and Okinawa), I meticulously examined stones at no less than ten different places. The old-style stones varied in weight from around 130 pounds up to about 260 pounds. Unlike modern weights, which are interchangeable, stone weights were fixed on a bar. Hence, I believe that few people then could lift more than Hercules Nakamura, as he became known.

A power lifting demonstration by Nakamura Shoei.

There can be no question that Nakamura is the strongest man in Okinawan history, and his international achievements are equalled only by Gushiken Yoko, another local boy who brought honor to Okinawa when he won the world boxing championships. Their accomplishments, and life stories, are certainly worthy of being perpetuated and, therefore, should also be passed down in future generations.

I invited Nakamura Shoei to our *dojo* on December 20, 1984, to give us a demonstration of his Herculean strength. We were all completely flabbergasted when he effortlessly ripped apart a two-inch-thick telephone book. It was obvious just how much strength he had. However, Nakamura was unable to break a one-and-a-half-inch-thick piece of green bamboo that we were using for a New Year's decoration with his grip strength.

Nakamura provided an explanation as to why he was unable to perform such a feat. He maintained that it was virtually impossible to crush such an object with grip strength alone. He even went as far as to say that nine times out of ten a piece of bamboo would probably remain unscathed even if a five-ton car ran over it! Judging by Nakamura's explanation, it would then seem quite unlikely that any karate master of old would have been able to accomplish such a feat. Notwithstanding, I was very appreciative to have someone as famous as Nakamura Shoei respond to our invitation and show the "proof of power."

The ten biographies introduced in this modest publication represent only a few of the principal experts of karate history. There are many many more, and I have every intention of making in depth studies of them as well. However, there were at least three masters whom I did not mention at length in this book who were, in no small way, responsible for making significant contributions to the development of modern karate-do: Uechi Kanbun, who founded Uechi-ryu; Chibana Choshin, who founded Kobayashi-ryu; and Miyagi Chojun, who founded Goju-ryu. One reason for this oversight was simply because there is no shortage of information surrounding these important men and I did not want to be redundant.

There are probably a million people in Japan who actively take part in the practice of karate. An Okinawan tradition which has drifted from our tiny shores to the four corners of the world, karate-do is really something at which to marvel. Now, as I look back over my long life, I can't help but feel fortunate to have been, if only in some small way, a part of it all.

We must continue to research and analyze this profound tradition, its history, philosophy, and application so that it becomes possible to establish a curriculum for transmitting its common principles. In that way the next generation can take karate-do to even greater heights.

Chapter 12

KEN ZEN ICHINYO
(KARATE AND ZEN ARE ONE)

THROUGH TRUE KARATE ONLY, CAN INNER PEACE BE FOUND

Karate is the product of an ongoing synthesis which had taken place over many generations here in Okinawa, an island of such tiny proportions when compared to the rest of the world. Nearly five centuries ago, Okinawa established both a peaceful and prosperous society through commerce and trade with China and Southeast Asia. It was in the second Sho Dynasty, during the reign of Shoshin (1477–1526), that Okinawa's trade with foreign countries reached its zenith. It was also a time when Shoshin established Okinawa's first centralized (civilian) government, which prohibited the private ownership and stockpiling of weapons, and forced local aristocrats to reside within the confines of Shuri castle. Okinawa enacted such mandates 150 years before the military government of Tokugawa (Edo Bakufu) ever considered such a policy.

The author practicing zazen. The calligraphy reads "One fist, ageless."

Buddhism also rose to its greatest height in Okinawa during that time and nearly 100 temples were ultimately erected throughout the archipelago. With the principal temples located in the castle district of Shuri, the majority belonged to the Rinzai Zen sect from Kansai, where the famous Kyoto Gozan (Five Temples of Kyoto) were located.

Among the most respected Zen priests of that era were Kaou and Nanyoshokou (also known as Chatan Choro, or Old Man of Chatan). It was also during Shoshin's reign in the early 1500s that the custom of loyally following one's master to the grave was prohibited. That was 158 years before a similar law was enacted by Japan's military government in 1663.

It is entirely possible that this sixteenth-century decree may have had some influence on martial arts philosophy, as an interesting proverb is said to have been developed after it was enacted. *"Tenoijira ijihiki ijinoijira tehiki"* means "if you become angry enough to strike out with your hands, use your mind to calm yourself down. If you lose your temper hold back your hands. You must always be patient and never hurt people. One can always sleep well even if one has been a victim of someone else's anger. However, it is difficult to sleep on a guilty conscience. Therefore, one should never harm another."

In 1882, Bushi Matsumura, the martial arts stalwart who faithfully served no fewer than three separate kings, wrote the "Seven Virtues of *Bu*," a document which had a profound impact on the philosophical development of karate-do. They are as follows:

1. *Bu* forbids wilful violence.
2. *Bu* governs the warrior.
3. *Bu* fortifies people.
4. *Bu* fosters virtue.
5. *Bu* appeases the community.
6. *Bu* brings about a general harmony.
7. *Bu* encourages prosperity.

Another ancient precept, first uttered by the founder of the Buddhist Rinzai sect, Muso Soseki, that prohibits violence became popularized by Funakoshi Gichin when he wrote *"Karate ni sente nashi"* (there is no first attack in karate).

Looking back over the development of karate in Okinawa, we can see how the prosperous commerce of the Ryukyu Kingdom attracted many foreign cultures to the shores of this tiny island after Shohashi finally unified the rival principalities. Through our subsequent contact with China and other foreign cultures, fighting principles were continually synthesized and assimilated into local combative traditions, thus enhancing their effectiveness. Such techniques were culti-vated by law enforcement officials and were also vigorously embraced by some wealthy landowners, but only after the private ownership and stockpiling of weapons were prohibited.

With the Satsuma samurai subjugating Okinawa militarily in 1609, we can see why it became important to cultivate such weapon-less defensive skills. With the prohibition of weapons, the develop-ment and mastery of empty-hand techniques became the necessary alternative. On the one hand, it was purely by chance that such a pro-found defensive tradition ascended and was handed down in such his-torical circumstances. Yet, on the other hand, under the weight of Satsuma's restrictions on religious practices, the tradition failed to properly incorporate and emphasize spiritual principles.

Zen philosophy had a profound impact on the development of martial arts on mainland Japan. However, in the old Ryukyu Kingdom it had little if any impact on local self-defense disciplines because of Satsuma's prohibition on such practices. For example, *shingitai* (mind, technique, and body) is the ideal training precept for martial arts, but, in the case of the pre-Meiji Okinawans, little emphasis was placed on such spiritual practices *(shin)* because of harsh political restrictions. To recognize this historical phenomenon is to understand how and why such overemphasis was placed on physical conditioning and practical application. By the time of the Meiji (1868–1912) and Taisho (1912–25) periods, karate training, a discipline void of the spiritual ele-ment, came to reflect this physical orientation. Most, if not all, teachers of karate placed more emphasis on *kakedameshi* (fighting) than they ever did on the inward journey. In spite of disliking such practices, I first learned karate under these circumstances.

MUSASHI AND TESHU BOTH TAUGHT THE SIGNIFICANCE OF ZEN

I took my first lesson in karate in 1923 when I was seventeen years old under the tutelage of Shimabuku Taro. Within three years I received a recommendation to study directly under Arakaki Ankichi, thanks to Shimabuku Senpai. Through diligent effort I not only came to improve my health and general fitness, but built considerable self-esteem and gained a new direction in life.

After passing my military medical and physical examinations with flying colors, I faithfully served my country until I was honorably dis-charged in 1931. Becoming a prefectural policemen provided me with the time and opportunity to pursue karate. It was during that time that I decided to dedicate my life to karate-do, and since that time I have never missed a practice.

Based at the Naha Central Police Station during WW II, I was appointed to be platoon leader in charge of emergency supplies. During that period I was sent from Shuri to the south of Shimajiri, where soldiers were engaged in a hard-fought battle. Under the smoke of an artillery barrage I was ultimately taken prisoner by the United States Army on the 22nd of June, 1945. During the time that I was a prisoner, I worked transporting wounded soldiers from the field. One day, quite by accident, I found two books on the street. One was *Karate-do Kyohan* by Funakoshi Gichin, the other was *Shikon* by Nakasaki Tatsukuro. During such adverse social circumstances, reading the philosophy of those two books had a profound impact on the way I came to embrace the martial arts with respect to the underlying moral philosophy.

In postwar Okinawa, I continued working for the police department and was transferred several times and received several promotions. Ascending to the position of chief of police, I finally retired in January of 1952 to open my school of karate in Naha's Kumoji district, where I have remained ever since. With the central populated areas of Okinawa being reduced virtually to rubble, thousands dead, and little or no social community left, crime was rampant.

I became terribly lonely in postwar Okinawa until I finally came to experience an inner emptiness which I had not previously known. It was during that introspective period that I began to reevaluate the teaching policy of karate with regard to its philosophy. In spite of the two profound training precepts hanging on the wall of my dojo, which read *"Karate ni sente nashi,"* and *"Mazu sono kokoro o seisu"* (Forge the spirit first), I must admit that I was far from embracing such a spirit. In the book *Shikon* (The Soul of the Samurai), I studied the works of Musashi Miyamoto and Tesshu Yamaoka. However, because I was not yet mentally prepared to understand the magnitude of their writings, it had no great impact on me at the time.

The following ten years passed rather quickly, bringing me no closer to enlightenment than I had previously been. However, after having read Musashi's *Gorin no Sho* (The Book of Five Rings) and Yamaoka's *Tesshu Ishi no Shinmenmoku* (Tesshu Proves His True Value), I gained enormous insight, renewed my own direction in life, and realized how karate should be taught in the future.

Musashi and Tesshu were both well-known swordsmen in Japanese history. Musashi was a product of the early Edo period (early- to mid-1600s), while Tesshu lived from the end of the *Bakufu* into the time when Japan was emancipated from feudalism (mid- to late-1800s). In spite of their social and chronological circumstances being quite different, both Musashi and Yamaoka were remarkable swordsmen who balanced their physical training with metaphysical precepts as a single practice. Moreover, it was through the introspective power cultivated in Zen Buddhism that they came to fully understand the secrets of martial arts. Although Musashi and Yamaoka both possessed enormous physical strength and remarkable technical skills, they recognized that true mastery could only ascend from defeating the greatest adversary of all: the enemy within. Coming to understand that the real obstacle was actually internal and not external, both Musashi and Yamaoka vigorously pursued an inward journey until they ultimately emerged reborn. Discovering the inward significance of such a profound practice, I resolved to not only to embrace *zazen* in my daily life, but also to introduce it into my *dojo* as a required study.

After having practiced *zazen* on my own for some time, I was able to receive three months of special training from the Zen priest Sakiyama Sogen, beginning in November of 1969. I remember learning that a Zen priest named Dogen, who lived during Japan's early Kamakura period, once said, "If you really wish it will come true." After my special training, I went to study under Okamoto Keisei, a Zen priest at the Reigen Temple in Okinawa's Itoman district. Afterwards, I started a *zazen* group and we have

Zazen should be mandatory training.

enjoyed regular Sunday morning training every week for many years now. From the Rinzai sect, our group is called Regein Hanazonokai and has about forty active members. When I first introduced the practice of *zazen* in my *dojo* most of the students complained about it. It took about three years before they finally got used to its practice. In the practice of *zazen,* it is said that "if one sits down a little bit at a time, one will find their Buddha nature a little bit at a time." Sitting in the *zazen seiza* (posture) for periods of fifteen minutes often presents physical difficulties which prevent easy concentration. *Zazen* is a quiet but severe practice, a practice through which one finds oneself. *Zazen* is the training of the *kokoro,* the mind. In the training precept known as *Shingitai, shin* represents *kokoro,* or the mind. In *budo* there is an expression "*Dō mu gen,*" which means "There is no end to learning." Death is the final lesson in our physical lives. Hence, it is only through cultivating the *kokoro* that *budo* can be totally understood.

To date there are many *karateka* who believe that the precept of *"karate ni sente nashi"* (there is no first attack in karate) is simply an unrealistic belief. This train of thought maintains that the prin- cipal of self-defense should be

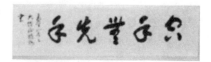

Calligraphy of "karate ni sente nashi" hanging in the author's *dojo*.

based on more sound reasoning. It also insists that the philosophical precept was contrived only to prohibit unwarranted violence. This point of view also concludes that the first move means certain victory. With that in mind I would now like to introduce my own opinion surrounding such a concept.

After a few years of *zazen* practice and lectures, I asked Master Okamoto Keisei if the precept of *"karate ni sente nashi"* was some kind of paradoxical question, not unlike the *koan* of Zen, where one con- templates its meaning in an effort to become illuminated.

The master priest instantly agreed. "Yes," he said, "it is a provoca- tive question for *karateka* captured by the essence of introspection, through which its meaning provides the essence of the tradition." I jumped for joy listening to his answer, as I had never heard that from any teacher of karate before.

In the history of Buddhism, its founder, Shakyamuni, was born 2500 years ago the son of a powerful king in one of India's many ancient kingdoms. In spite of being brought up in wealth and posi- tion, he came to renounce the world at twenty-nine years of age. In so doing, his goal was to help resolve human suffering. Following six long and hard years of embracing asceticism, Shakyamuni was spiri- tually awakened one day while sitting under a Bodhi tree. From that time forward, Shakyamuni set forth to teach the world and continued his untiring efforts for forty-five years until his great awakening and death, through which he entered *Maha-Pari-Nirvana*.

Buddha's teachings are aimed at transcending ego-related distrac- tions and cultivating the world within in an effort to enhance the world without. The mind is a microcosm of the universal macrocosm, and Zen is one school of Buddhist thought through which this truth can be attained. "Although there are many paths which lead up a mountain, there is only one moon to be seen by all those who achieve its summit," a Zen saying goes. Cultivating indomitable fortitude is a necessary prerequisite for any and all *budoka* who aspire to transcend the immediate results of physical training and overcome the source of human weakness and suffering. Needless to say, it is through such inner achievement that one can become impervious to abusive provocation, and hence never be reduced to physical violence.

If one considers Japanese martial arts in general, especially its competitive interpretation, one will quickly discover that great lip-service is placed on the importance of such precepts like *"shingitai-ichinyo."* However, in reality little if any emphasis is ever actually placed on such precepts on the mainland of Japan, or here in Okinawa, for that matter!

If one never gets beyond the immediate results of physical *(gitai)* training, the precept of *"karate ni sente nashi"* can never be completely understood. When one is trapped by dualism, Zen is one way to escape the bondage of such inner conflict. Through Zen one can come not only to recognize the real meaning of *"karate ni sente nashi,"* but can also understand how the mind represents a microcosm of the Universe, and discover the infinite connection between all of creation. We humans tend to ignore that which we cannot see, touch, or feel. We are creatures of greed and materialism.

After many years of searching for testimony which connected Zen to karate, I finally received a letter from Kuniyoshi Yukie, a highly regarded authority of Ryukyu history. In his letter I was pleased to learn that the Gokokuji, a Shingon Buddhist temple, had been erected in the Naminoue district of Naha's Kume village in 1368 by a monk named Yorishige. The temple grounds also served as the location on which Okinawa's "thirty-six Chinese families" later established the Tenson Mausoleum. With Kume village being the window of Chinese culture in Okinawa, the mausoleum housed many valuable documents about the politics, economy, religion, and military science of the Middle Kingdom. Among the many documents on military science, there was the Wu Bei Zhi (*Bubishi* in Japanese), an important text which contains the maxims of Sun Tzu, and "The Eight Phrases of *Chuan Fa* (*kenpo* in Japanese). However, with the bombing of the Tenson Mausoleum during the war, its contents were destroyed.

Ultimately, I did come to study "The Eight Phrases of *Chuan Fa,*" which I was able to locate from an alternative source. However, having only superficially read through it, without truly understanding the *"karate ni sente nashi"* precept, I couldn't actually grasp its deepest meaning. Yet, having vigorously practiced *zazen* for so long, I remember how deeply moved I was after re-reading the document. Discovering and then cultivating one's world within establishes such clarity and insight that mastery of karate is simply not possible without it.

Chapters one through three in this book discuss *kokoro,* whereas chapters four through seven address the *gitai* phenomenon. Listed below are three precepts from "The Eight Phrases of *Chuan Fa*" as they appear in the ancient *Bubishi*. They are identical to the Zen philosophy which maintains that "the human mind is a microcosm of the universal macrocosm."

1. The human mind is one with heaven and earth.
2. Our blood circulation parallels the solar and lunar cycles of each day.
3. Inhalation represents softness; exhalation characterizes hardness.

I believe it is safe to conclude that the connection between Zen and martial arts dates back far into Chinese history. However, as I mentioned before, because of the Satsuma prohibition on religion, Buddhist practices as observed in old Okinawa were reduced purely to rituals for birth and death. In the case of defensive traditions, I'm afraid that there was little or no emphasis ever placed on spirituality, and the martial arts were perpetuated through its *gitai,* or physical rituals only.

DEDICATED TO SEEKING KEN ZEN ICHINYO

It has only been in the last half century that karate has gone from the sandy shores of our tiny island community to the four corners of the world. In fact, Okinawan karate is now practiced in numerous countries around the world. It has been a remarkable experience to have witnessed the rapid growth and proliferation of karate in my lifetime. Its competition manifestations and subsequent commercial exploitation have given rise to a myriad of "new" methods. As such, the body of moral philosophy which serves to govern the behavior of those who learn the secrets of the ancient masters has all but vanished in the trail of eclectic interpretations. Except in very rare cases, it appears that the inward journey of karate-do has been overshadowed by pursuits of less rewarding value. During a generation so dominated by greed and preoccupied by materialism, modern karate seems to be hampered by the very issues that it seeks to eradicate.

Void of its spiritual foundation, karate is reduced to common brutality. It is of the utmost importance that physical training be balanced by philosophical assimilation and methodical introspection as a single practice. In bringing the karate section of this text to an end, I would like to leave the reader with something to ponder:

In my lifetime I came to learn the significance of *"ken zen ichinyo."* Having learned the spiritual essence of karate-do through embracing the true precepts of *shingitai,* I am a true advocate of Zen, a tradition which has a 2500 year history. I believe that the value of mastering karate lies not in physical superiority, but rather social pliability—learning to live in harmony with nature and one's fellow man rather than frivolously trying to dominate or destroy. Grasping the value of each and every moment of one's life as if it were the last requires a clarity of thought not commonly associated with simple physical pursuits. Most people go through life regretting the past, fearing the future, and missing the moment. Not really considering myself a master, I have remained faithful to the inward journey cultivated through this profound tradition. In doing so, I continue to enjoy the peaceful rewards made possible through the daily pursuit of karate-do, Okinawa's unique cultural asset.

Chapter 13

BASIC INSTRUCTION FOR ZAZEN

The following explanation of *zazen* was made possible through the courtesy of Tenshin Tanouye Rotaishi, Archbishop of the Daihonzan Chozen-ji/International Zen Dojo in Honolulu, Hawaii.

To sit *zazen* well, one must harmonize mind, body, and breath. Only when the three are realized as one will it be possible to succeed in stabilizing and tranquilizing the body and mind at the same time. Each of these three things is inseparably related to the other two.

Beginners tend to overstrain the area of the lower abdomen because of the emphasis put there. Each individual is different in his physical structure and so must guide himself accordingly. One should sit in such a way as to cause his energy to pervade the

The author in a sitting zazen posture.

whole body instead of forcing himself to put physical pressure in the lower abdomen.

It is important to wear clothes that are loose enough for good circulation. It is also important to look neat; there must be dignity in appearance to establish the proper mood for sitting.

As *zazen* is not a test of quiet endurance, it is meaningless to sit for long periods without concentrating and unifying the mind and body. Thirty or forty minutes—the time one incense stick takes to burn—is adequate for beginners. Of course, five or ten minutes will be enough if we sit fully and seriously. The crucial point is the degree of concentration rather than the length of sitting.

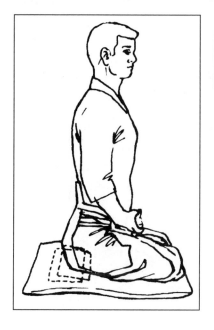

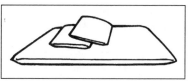

PLACEMENT OF CUSHIONS

Select a wide cushion and two or three small ones. Stack the smaller ones on top of the wide one so they act as a wedge. Sit with the buttocks placed near the center of the top cushion.

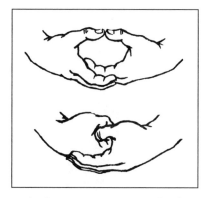

POSITIONS OF THE HANDS

In the first position shown, the left hand is placed palm up so that it rests on the palm of the right hand. The inner sides of the tips of both thumbs touch, creating an ellipse. Viewed from above, the thumbs must be in line with the middle fingers.

The more common position is the bottom one. Grasp the first joint of the left thumb between the web of the thumb and the index finger of the right hand. Form a loose fist with the right hand and enclose it with the left.

To take the full lotus position, place the right foot on the left thigh and the left foot on the right thigh.

To take the half lotus position, place the right foot near the base of the left thigh and the left foot on the right thigh. (The legs can be reversed in both of these positions.)

Full lotus position

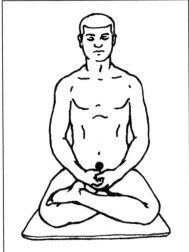

Half lotus position

STABILIZING THE BODY (FRONT VIEW)

A well-seated and very stable body is one in the form of a pyramid. The base is an imaginary triangle formed by the lines connecting the two knees and the coccyx. The diagonal ridge lines extending from the two knees and the coccyx to the top of the head complete the pyramid.

Rock the body from right to left and again from left to right. The amplitude of the oscillation should be large at first and gradually decrease until the body stops moving and becomes stable.

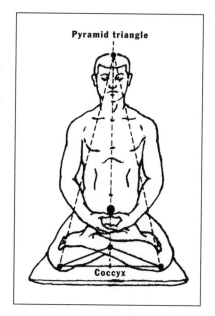

STABILIZING THE BODY (SIDE VIEW)

Straighten the spine perpendicularly by inclining the upper body forward. Then, push the buttocks backward without moving them while raising the upper body gradually as if to push heaven with the back of the head. This action will straighten the spine into a natural position.

Advance the lower abdomen forward to straighten the hips. Raise the upper body until it becomes perpendicular to the

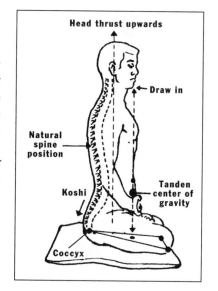

ground; the neck will be upright and the lower jaw will be drawn in. The center of gravity will now coincide with the geometrical center of the plane triangle.

Check and see that the lower jaw is drawn in and the back of the neck is straight. If they are in the correct position, the ears and shoulders should fall along the same perpendicular plane.

Check also the position of the lower abdomen and the hips. If the lower abdomen is forward and the hip bone is upright, the nose and navel should be aligned.

Let the tip of the tongue touch the roof of the mouth with the teeth in light contact with each other.

Sit at ease, heavy and in alert dignity like Mt. Fuji soaring into heaven and overlooking the Pacific Ocean.

ADJUSTING THE VISION

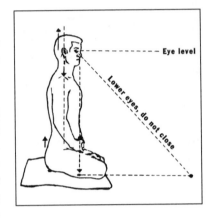

Adjusting the vision helps to focus attention and prevents it from being taken up by internal or external stimuli.

The eyes should look straight ahead, and the visual field should span 180 degrees. Lower the gaze to a fixed position on the floor approximately three feet ahead. The eyes should be half-closed in selfless tranquility, neither seeing nor not seeing anything.

Do not close your eyes. In order to enter the state of Zen concentration and to raise your inner power to the utmost, it is important to keep the eyes open. If you remain quiet with your eyes closed like lifeless water, you will never be useful to society. It may seem easier to unify yourself spiritually by closing the eyes, but then it will be inert *zazen*. Interpreting it more lightly, keeping your eyes open prevents you from falling asleep in meditation.

Deep breathing harmonizes the mind and body.

Exhale slowly through the mouth as if to connect the atmosphere with the lower abdomen. Empty all the stale air with the strength created by the contraction of the lower abdomen. At the end of exhalation, relax the lower abdomen.

Due to atmospheric pressure, new air will naturally enter through the nose and fill the vacuum in the lungs.

After inhaling fully, pause slightly. With the *koshi* (waist, hips) extended forward, gently push the inhaled air into the lower abdomen with a scooping motion. The key to this is to contract the sphincter muscle.

Start exhaling again just before you feel uncomfortable. Repeat this type of breathing four to ten times.

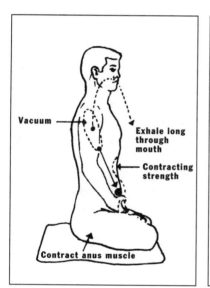
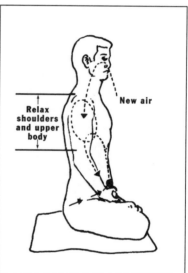

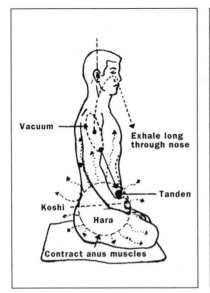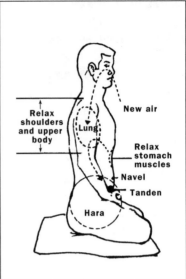

BREATHING IN MEDITATION

When the respiration is adjusted, start breathing naturally through the nose with the mouth closed. If you relax the muscles around the pit of the stomach as you inhale, it will feel as if air is filling the area below the navel.

Exhale through the nose. The breath should be long and directed toward the *tanden* with the muscles around the anus and push the hips upright and slightly forward. The power should feel as if coming out of the area below the navel. The concentration on the lower extremities of the body should relax the shoulders and the upper body.

Inhaling should be left to occur naturally as new air fills the vacuum in the lungs. In exhaling and inhaling, instead of using physical force, concentrate energy on the lower abdomen. Gradually, conscious effort will lessen and the frequency of breathing will naturally decrease. When the vital power is at the *tanden* and confined in the *hara* (abdomen), this spiritual strength and vital energy will radiate through the entire body.

Count your respiration with all of your spiritual power as if trying to penetrate to the core of the earth. Count the frequency of the exhalation from one to ten. Count in syllables as long as the exhalation. One, two, and so on. Let your mind's eye follow the exhaled air in counting. If you miscount before reaching the count of ten, or count beyond ten, start again from one.

In order to avoid incongruence between your respiration and the count, it is essential to concentrate your mind on the count, rather than on the respiration as such, and feel as if you are breathing in accordance with the count.

PART THREE

TEGUMI AND MASTER GRAPPLERS OF OKINAWA

CHAPTER 14

OKINAWAN TEGUMI

INTRODUCTION

When I was a child, like many children, I always felt at home with nature and enjoyed playing in the trees, fields, and streams. As children growing up in and around the Tomari district, we did such things as climb trees, throw stones, and play "king of the mountain" in the pine forests around Koganemori, Takamasari, and the Sogenji elevation. Covered in mud like eels, we swam in the Azato River. Sometimes in the evenings we also pretended we were fierce *tegumi* wrestlers and fought each other at the playground, in the pine forest, on temple grounds, or even in the caves. Hating school homework, I always looked forward to playing with my childhood friends. In spite of being quite small for my age, I was a leader among my friends and loved *tegumi* grappling with them.

In 1923, I first joined the judo club at the old commercial school, which fell under the jurisdiction of the prewar system in those days. There I met Ishikawa Seijin, who was senior to me by two grades. Besides being quite intelligent academically, he was very athletic and talented in many sports. Having won many judo and Okinawan sumo tournaments both at home and throughout the archipelago, Ishikawa was revered by us as a god. I often dreamed about how happy I would be if I only possessed just a fraction of his strength and skill.

When I finally realized that karate, when compared to the demands of judo and sumo, was more suitable for someone of my size and strength, I nearly stopped practicing other martial arts. That was during the second year of my commercial school studies. However, Arakaki Ankichi Sensei told me, "Of course you should concentrate primarily on your karate, but do not overlook the value of learning as much as you can about other kinds of martial arts and sports, too. In that way you will improve your fitness level, expand your range of knowledge in general, and also improve your ability to respond more effectively in self-defense." I took the advice of my sensei and practiced judo and sumo diligently during my days as a student.

I had a classmate Kushi Jokei, who became *yokozuna* (grand champion of Okinawan sumo) at the Naminoue festival of 1935. I found a kindred spirit in that man and respected his sumo philosophy. After graduation from the commercial school, we promised each other that, in spite of going our own ways, we would stay in contact with each other and continue to research the fighting traditions. From that time forth we always went to the sumo bouts together to study the techniques of other sumo wrestlers and enjoy the contests. Among those events I best remember were the Naminoue festival every May 17th, the Makishiugan festival on May 5th of the Chinese calendar, and the Shokon festival at Onoyama Park on October 23rd.

Kushi Jokei

After the war, Kushi organized the Okinawa Sumo Association in an effort to help improve Okinawa's depressed social atmosphere. The organization ultimately became recognized by the Okinawan Institution of Physical Education. Supportive of sumo president Kinjo Masayuki, Kushi's efforts were instrumental in establishing the foundation on which the current Okinawan sumo community unfolded. Additionally, Kushi was an avid historian and collected research material surrounding the origins and legends of Okinawan sumo. Sadly, my old friend fell sick and passed away before he could ever publish any of his research. Although I do not consider myself an expert in sumo, I was, nonetheless, Kushi's best friend and, since we graduated, carried an obligation I have never forgotten. With that in mind I would now like to conclude this book by presenting my friend's research. I hope that the reader will recognize my effort and appreciate its meaning.

TEGUMI AND THE ORIGINS OF OKINAWAN SUMO

The Japanese term *sumo*, as defined by the Kojirin dictionary, refers to two people grappling together in a ring. Originally grappling was used as a principal vehicle in martial arts to develop one's strength and promote well being. Later this unique form of grappling was cultivated as a cultural form of recreation for general amusement.

Actually, there are no accurate historical documents surrounding the origins of grappling in Okinawa. It is believed that grappling ascended from primitive man's instinctive means of self-preservation. In the history of civil fighting traditions here in Okinawa we refer to such grappling concepts as *tegumi*. There is every reason to believe that *tegumi*, after being enhanced by techniques of striking and kicking, also served as the progenitor of "*te*."

While the tradition was called *tegumi* in Naha, it was known as *mutou* in both Tomari and Shuri where it remained a popular cultural recreation until the Taisho period. In its early recreational form, *tegumi* was quite a rough and tumble practice. Notwithstanding, it is believed that the tradition was not completely unlike present day amateur wrestling where the victor is the one who conclusively defeats his opponent by twisting his joints, sealing his breath, or holding him down so that he can no longer move.

Since those early times, *tegumi* has been refined and a firm set of rules and regulations has been developed. It unfolded as popular cultural tradition and has been handed down to this day. According to island folklore, Okinawan sumo ascended from *tegumi*.

GATHERINGS, VENUES, AND THE SUMO RING

Because Okinawan sumo had never been promoted in the same spectacular way as its Japanese counterpart on Japan's mainland, islanders never bothered building permanent sumo rings or venues to host such local events or championships.

To the Okinawans of yesteryear, sumo wrestling had been an exciting cultural recreation for everyone to enjoy. It was not a commodity to be exploited in such grandeur. That is simply not the Okinawan way. In the old days, any open space, field, or mountainside where people could freely gather and watch in their own comfort was sufficient. During that time there were no special rules or regulations about the size or configuration of the ring. The only condition was that the grappling surface had to be free of small stones or anything else that might be of danger to the grapplers. Usually, such bouts took place on a lawn, or surface covered by sand or sawdust to ensure safety for the athletes.

Such events or championships were usually held on national holidays or cultural festivals. Okinawa has been plagued by typhoons and droughts for centuries. Such natural phenomena left destruction and famine in their wake. *Tegumi* (sumo) became a cultural tradition dedicated to the gods of heaven and earth for abundant harvests and bountiful fish catches.

Naha's Naminoue Sumo Tournament was originally held in mid-autumn on August 15th during the lunar calendar. However, the date later changed to May 17 of the solar calendar. *O-bon* (a festival commemorating the spirits of ancestors) is celebrated on the 16th of July of the lunar calendar with the Nakano Mou Sumo Tournament held on the following day. The Makishiugan Sumo Tournament was held on Boys'

The sumo ring at Naminoue.

Day (May 5th of the lunar calendar), and the Shokonasai Sumo Tournament was held on October 23rd at Onoyama Park.

In Shuri, such events were held at the Kannon-do (Buddhist Temple) during September 18th of the lunar calendar, and another popular tournament was always held at the memorial field during the Kensha festival on the 20th of October. In Mawashi, tournaments were held at Uedomaimo on August 16th of the lunar calendar. In Uroku, tournaments were held at Gushimo on both July 15th and August 15th of the lunar calendar.

After the war, most if not all of these sumo tournaments simply stopped because of the widespread destruction, a drastic change in lifestyles, and the enormity of the American military bases, which occupied the land on which many of the events were once held. However, a few tournaments continued on, such as the Naminoue Tournament, the Makishiugan Tournament, and the tournament at the Kannon-do, all of which remain even to this day. These days, Okinawan sumo seems to enjoy more popularity in outlying areas than it does in either Shuri or Naha.

DIFFERENCES BETWEEN OKINAWAN AND JAPANESE SUMO

In Okinawan sumo, *suninjima* is an expression which means "sumo audience participation," but actually refers to its attitude toward a biased referee or clumsy wrestler. In the days of old-style *tegumi*, referees scored each bout according to an unwritten standard. This helped establish a feeling of togetherness between audience, referee, and wrestler. In Okinawa, this feeling of togetherness is often described as *shurei*.

If a wrestler intentionally kicked his opponent, or struck him in the face using *"harite"* during a bout, it was regarded as common brutality and not *tegumi*. In such a case the audience would verbally abuse the wrestler according to the *"suninjima"* principle. Such infractions rarely if ever occurred. *Shimagashira*, or tournament directors, were usually selected from among the oldest or most senior retired wrestlers. Under the directors were the *gyoji*, or referees, and the *yobidashi*, or announcers. Often directors also served as referees and/or announcers.

The difference between Okinawan and Japanese sumo is reflected in size, manner of dress, and the fundamental engagement positions with respect to gripping the *mawashi* (belts). In Japanese sumo the contestants, dressed only in a *mawashi* and often enormous in weight, usually charge into each other with tremendous force in an effort to fight for a dominant position and grip. In Okinawa sumo, such tactics are not used and the contestant's jacket and pants are supported by the *mawashi*. There are differences in judging as well. For example, wrestlers are not penalized for going outside the ring or falling to the ground as they are in Japanese sumo. A bout is over only when the contestant falls on his back inside the ring. Additionally, a wrestler today must not twist the opponent's joints, grasp the collar, pull out his legs, push him down, or even use the hands to prevent the application of an opponent's technique during a bout. To know that Okinawan sumo had never been promoted in the same spectacular way that it was on Japan's mainland is to understand why little publicity has ever surrounded its tournaments.

MASTER DIRECTORS, REFEREES, AND ANNOUNCERS OF OKINAWAN SUMO

Prominent *shimagashira* of the Meiji (1868-1911) and Taisho (1911-1926) periods included Yabu "the Sergeant" Kentsu (1866-1937), Hanashiro "the Sergeant" Chomo (1869–1945), Tomihara (Yamato) Seiyu (1874–1930), and Ono Sakae (1886–?).

Yabu Kentsu   Hanashiro Chomo   Tomihara (Yamato)   Ono Sakae
                                          Seiyu

Prominent referees and announcers from the Taisho to early Showa (1926–1989) periods included Oshiro Ankei (1882–1931), Takayasu Koujun (1888–1953), and Tomoyose Eigen (1900–1980). Yabu and Hanashiro, both ex-soldiers and senior masters of karate, were also still active during that time. Ono Sakae was a teacher at the Naha Commercial School, and Tomihara was a well-known actor and *bujin*. Oshiro was employed as a school faculty member, Takayasu was part of the prefectural assembly, and Tomoyose was a dentist.

PRINCIPAL TECHNIQUES OF OKINAWAN SUMO

Established in 1956, the following terms replaced pre-war terms: *koshi* (hip technique); *nushi* (right and left); *watanushi* (right and left); *hichinushi* (right and left); *meegaki* (right and left); *uchi meegaki* (right and left); *finushi* (right and left); *machi* (right and left); *ashi harai* (right and left); *hiza guruma* (right and left); and *ten meegaki* (right and left), and so on. Other techniques excluded here are identical to those of judo.

Chapter 15

BIOGRAPHIES OF OKINAWAN TEGUMI MEIJIN

The history of old-style *tegumi* is filled with splendid tales of masters who possessed incredible strength and physical prowess. For example, the tales of Itoman Magi and Oshima Magi of Motobu are known to many and have become folklore among locals. However, in spite of enjoying certain popularity, we must remember that these tales are just that, stories handed down by word of mouth and must be considered legends of sorts. The actual lives and personalities of such men remain a mystery. With that in mind, I would like to introduce two well-known *meijin* from the mid-Meiji Period.

AKARIE MATSUZO (1889–1922)

Matsuzo was born in 1889 in Akarie, Aza, Nago village, Kunikamigun and, like many *Uchinanchu* (Okinawans), travelled with his father to live in Hawaii. When he was 21 years old he returned to Okinawa to enlist in the Japanese military, despite having spent so many years in a foreign country. Passing his physical with flying colors, Akarie was a towering 6

Akarie Matsuzo

feet tall, weighed 188 pounds and was in incredible physical condition, with remarkable muscularity. Akarie was described as an all-round athlete, with a light complexion and rather handsome.

As I mentioned previously, the Naminoue Tournament, held on

May 17th, was the biggest sumo event in Okinawa at that time. Every year spectators from all over the archipelago came to watch. So popular was the Naminoue Tournament that if one did not get there the morning before the event, one could not get a good position to see the matches. To add more confusion to the annual chaos, rarely, if ever, did the tournament get started on time. Hordes of people always obstructed the roadways and lined the stone walls around the temples at Naminoue, Saikoujiyama, and Gokokuji.

The dream of every wrestler in those days was to one day win the Naminoue Tournament and the excitement in the air was always thick enough to cut with a sword. For many, the tournament was more than just the opportunity to compete against the very best in the Ryukyus. It was the chance to be the undisputed champion of Okinawa, the chance of a lifetime.

Preparing to compete in this monumental event, Akarie Matsuzo had trained diligently, and, in doing so, even abstained from having sex with his wife for one month before the tournament. On the day of the tournament he performed the ritual of cleansing his new sumo *gi* in the smoke of burning incense at his family altar. Actually, he reminded me in many ways of 1984 Los Angeles Olympic judo gold medalist Yamashita Yasuhiro. The king of judo, he too was a man who prepared three of his own judo *gi* for his participation in the Olympic games in the same way. In preparing to go beyond that which was expected of them, these stalwarts clearly reflected their indomitable spirit and regard for ancient ritual and tradition. I remain impressed by men of that caliber in spite of the era and circumstances being completely different. To me the principles remain the same.

A traditional fighter, Matsuzo employed the fundamental postures of Okinawan sumo and favored a left and right *hichichinushi*. Remaining undefeated in three consecutive bouts, he was unrivaled. In spite of some people screaming for his defeat, it never happened. The audience was alive with anticipation as Matsuzo went on to claim victory after victory, ultimately emerging as the champion of Okinawa.

Matsuzo contracted pneumonia and died on February 4, 1922 at the incredibly young age of thirty-four. I remember hearing that Yabu Kentsu, who was a popular *shimagashira* at that time, mourned Akarie's death as if he were his own son. Master Yabu said at his funeral that "There will never be another wrestler like Matsuzo." After his death the people of Akarie village immortalized his spirit by regarding him as the patron saint of victory in athletic competition. Before a competition in Nago village it became a custom of sorts for athletes to pray for victory with their teammates at Matsuzo's tomb.

Around 1976, while researching the history of this great man, I visited the Matsuzo home and met with the late Akarie Matsuzo's wife. She enjoyed speaking about her husband and fondly remembered old times. After leaving her home, I went to Akarie Matsuzo's final resting place, quietly burned incense, joined my palms together, and prayed for the spirit of that great man.

HAWAII'S KAWASAKI VS OKINAWA'S KINJO: THE CONFRONTATION

KAWASAKI KITATSU

Kawasaki Kitatsu was born in 1897, in Okinawa's Heian-za, Nakagami district. In the Taisho Period, after graduating from Okinawa's Prefectural Second Junior High School, he, like many other *Uchinanchu* his age, travelled to Hawaii to find work.

Kawasaki Kitatsu

Tall for an Okinawan, he was unrivaled in power as a student, and especially strong as a wrestler. Additionally, Kawasaki learned karate directly under the tutelage of the great master Yabu Kentsu. He was also quite good at English, which gave him an edge for living in a foreign country such as Hawaii.

In Hawaii, he was known by his nickname "Kawasaki Magi." In those days it was fashionable for young men seeking a new future to emigrate to Hawaii. Sumo caught on there and was naturally enjoyed by many in the Okinawan community. Kawasaki's name became very well known, as every time there was a tournament he won. At 5 feet, 10 inches tall and a robust 176 pounds, Kawasaki went virtually undefeated for a couple of years in his bid to remain the undisputed champion of *tegumi* in Hawaii. During that time he was the king of sumo in Hawaii.

In early 1935, he visited Okinawa for the first time in many years. During his trip he dropped in to visit the local newspaper offices. There he talked about the popularity of sumo in Hawaii and his competitive success. During his presentation Kawasaki suggested that the newspaper consider sponsoring a match between him and Okinawa's strongest wrestler at the time.

The newspaper accepted his idea and petitioned Tomoyose Eigen to consider organizing the match. Although he could not accept the responsibility of organizing the event, he did introduce Miyagi Sanpei from the Naha Police Department. In addition to being a policeman, Miyagi had won the Naminoue Tournament and was an ideal candidate for the match. However, Miyagi refused right away on the grounds that Kinjo Masayuki was far superior to him and that it should be a man of comparable skill—Kinjo Masayuki—to accept such a challenge.

In an effort to have Kinjo accept the challenge, Tomoyose wrote to him at the Sakimotobu Elementary School, where he worked. However, Kinjo's reply indicated that he would be unable to accept the offer, much to his dismay, as his mother had prohibited him from wrestling ever again. Unable to accept that decision, Tomoyose immediately visited Kinjo's home and negotiated a successful agreement.

With the notice of the match finally being published in the local newspaper, it became the talk of the town, and fans got really excited. In spite of the two men hailing from the districts of Kunikami and Nakagami, the bout was billed as "Hawaii vs. Okinawa" and enormous teams of male cheerleaders were formed to support both sides.

KINJO MASAYUKI

Kinjo Masayuki was born in Sakimotobu in 1904 and, since childhood, excelled in combative sports. He liked grappling and was naturally gifted, extremely flexible, and was incredibly strong. In an effort to improve his strength and overall condition Kinjo constructed an enormous heavy bag. When he trained, he tied his belt to the middle of the bag and sparred with it for hours every day. Additionally, he trained

Kinjo Masayuki

with stone weights many times daily. Iraha Chosei, a teacher and member of the Okinawan Track and Field Association, told me that Kinjo was unrivaled in Kunikami and regarded as the king of *tegumi* in his district by the time he was twenty-five or twenty-six years old. Iraha also said that Kinjo ultimately became recognized as the best wrestler in all of Okinawa. With a muscular 5 foot, 9 inch frame, Kinjo carried his 165 pounds with perfect balance and, according to Iraha, was admired by every youth in Okinawa at that time.

It was decided that the unprecedented match was to be held at the annual Shokonsai Festival in Onoyama Park. Heading up Kawasaki's male cheerleaders were Dr. Shimojo Eishin, an ophthalmologist, and Tsukenjo Kamechiki, who gathered their forces together at the residence of Nishimiya Teiichi, owner of the Heian-za inn. Kinjo's male cheerleaders were organized by Uema Tokinosuke, the chairman of the prefectural assembly, and Kohama Fushisuke, the deputy of Motobu village. Together these men gathered at the Shodokan, which at the time was managed by Itokazu Shoko, the judo sensei of Okinawa's First Junior High School.

After preparing their teams the leaders paraded down to Onoyama Park with flags waving and drums beating. Along the way they were joined by excited fans and enthusiastic bystanders. As they converged onto Onoyama Park they were met by hordes of excited people amidst the waving flags, blowing whistles, and furious drums.

The undercard bouts featured wrestlers like Iraha Chosei and Hekishiki Zentoku. Hekishiki, who imparted this story to me, is presently the chairman of the Okinawan Track and Field Association. By the time the main event was ready to start, the *shimagashira,* Hanashiro Chomo, and others took their positions alongside as the two big wrestlers faced each other in the center of the ring. As Takayasu Koshun, the referee, stepped into the ring with the red and-white flags, Tomoyose Eigen, the announcer, introduced the two wrestlers. The two adversaries, Kawasaki Kitatsu, thirty-nine years old, and Kinjo Masayuki, thirty-two years old, bowed to each other and shook hands. It was very dramatic as the three round match got under way.

The Kawasaki and Kinjo match.

As the combatants engaged it was so silent you could hear a pin drop. The match went back and forth and the audience was not disappointed by the intensity or the skill of either man. Unfortunately, the fighting was brought to an unexpected end when, during the intense bout, Kawasaki fell down on his shoulder, breaking his collar bone, and had to be rushed to the hospital.

That was in 1934 when I was working at the Naha police station. I remember watching this match with my friend Kushi Jokei. We were flabbergasted by the combatants' huge bodies and tremendous technique. I'll never forget that match nor the words of Miyagi Sanpei. My colleague at the police department, Miyagi carried 190 pounds on a 6 foot frame and had been a consecutive champion of the Naminoue Sumo Tournament. Miyagi said "One must know one's strengths and weaknesses, there is always someone better. I would have been no match for Kinjo."

In spite of the match ending under such unfortunate circumstances, the men's indomitable spirit and intensity made for a dramatic presentation. Both were great wrestlers and, in my humble opinion, no one can better those men in the future of this native tradition.

After the war Kawasaki Kitatsu became an interpreter for the military and went on to become the mayor of Yonashiro village. He passed away at the age of sixty-six. Kinjo Masayuki became a school principal, an accountant for the Ryukyu Government, and ultimately the town mayor of Motobu. He passed away at the age of seventy-seven. In retrospect, I have fond memories of those men and the kind people that they were. I often think about the contributions that they made to our culture and hope that they are resting in peace.

UEZU AND ISHIKAWA: A CONFRONTATION OF SMALL WRESTLERS

UEZU JIRYO

Uezu Jiryo was born on the 10th of September 1900 in Kumejima's (Kume island) Gushikawa village. Because the island was so isolated from the rest of the archipelago, few if any modern sports were ever promoted there during his youth. However, as *tegumi* was the most popular sport in all of Okinawa, and could be performed virtually anywhere, boys often gathered together to play on the sandy beach, the street, or in a field. Uezu grew up learning under such circumstances.

Uezu Jiryo

Going to school in Okinawa under the old system, Uezu was a bright young scholar who also excelled in physical fitness. He was especially talented in wrestling and regarded as a force to be reckoned with. In fact, after considerable training and tournament victories, there was no one who could beat him in and around the old castle district of Shuri. He carried his muscular 132 pounds on a 5 foot, 3 inch frame as if he were twice as heavy. He was fast and flexible, and many believed that his reflexes were beyond compare.

After graduating at the top of his class from the teacher's college, Uezu Jiryo was recruited as a teacher for the elementary school connected to Okinawa's Women's Teacher College. Within a couple of years he was transferred to Azato Elementary School, where he then served as the principal. Yet, it was through teaching at Azato that Uezu ultimately discovered his desire to pursue higher learning. Having procured a new posting on the mainland, Uezu was to leave for Tokyo the following April, where he would later enter the university in an effort to continue his own studies. Hence, the forthcoming match against Ishikawa would, win or lose, represent his retirement bout.

ISHIKAWA SEIJIN

Ishikawa Seijin

Ishikawa Seijin was born in 1905 in Kamimotobu's Jabana village in the Kunikamigun district. Kunikamigun was an area in which warrior traditions were vigorously cultivated by the once powerful Ganko political party, which used to rally there during the end of the Ryukyu Kingdom (ca. 1879). Seijin's father, Seikun, a man well known for this *kunikamigun* (in this case it means "fighting spirit"), had once been regarded as the best sumo wrestler in his village, fighting under the nickname "Bogani." It was under Spartan circumstances that a young Ishikawa Seijin was trained in the native discipline of *tegumi*.

In April of 1921, he entered the Naha Commercial School. Like Kumejima's Uezu, Ishikawa was intelligent and highly regarded by his peers. Excelling in both athletics and academic studies, he soon became his class leader. Also like Uezu, Ishikawa was quite small, in fact, nearly identical to him in both size and ability. Ishikawa was so talented that he was referred to as the "wonder-kid" throughout his school life. Many say he should have become a gymnast because he was so good at tumbling. Others maintained that his judo and wrestling were superior simply because no one could ever defeat him. Once, during the peak of his popularity, and in spite of his small size, he defeated ten men in a row, all much bigger than he was.

It was during the fifth year of Commercial School that Ishikawa took his physical examination for military service. Passing with flying colors, he was scheduled to be drafted following graduation. Hence, the opportunity to face an opponent of Uezu's caliber was an ideal retirement match for Ishikawa, too.

It was the twentieth of October 1925, during the crowded Kensha Festival at Shuri Memorial Field, that the two combatants, Uezu and Ishikawa, finally met each other. Secretly they had trained diligently for this match, their retirement tournament. Right from the beginning Ishikawa appeared ready and eager to engage his famous opponent. So too did Uezu look completely confident. Both stalwarts had every intention of ending the match victoriously, and it was such spirit that made the atmosphere of that event so intense.

THE MATCH

With the excited throngs of people, all one could hear by the time the match finally got under way was whistling, feverish clapping, loud cheering, and the wild beat of the drums. Bursting at the seams, the crowd was alive with anticipation. Both men viciously seized for *migiyotsu*[16] and moved aggressively fighting for superiority. The bout was hot and furious as both men moved in and out of potentially hazardous encounters. Five minutes passed, then ten. The audience forgot itself, breathlessly basking in awe of the gladiator-style combat. Regardless of which way or how powerful a technique was delivered it was countered with equal ferocity. The bout continued on until the decision was made to call the match a draw. The audience agreed and the tie was an outstanding conclusion to the careers of those remarkable

The Uezu and Ishikawa match.

grapplers. Enthusiasts remained at the venue for some time after the bout discussing the strategies and techniques of both combatants. Uezu was twenty-six years old, Ishikawa just twenty-one.

Though Uezu was older than Ishikawa by five years, they were both in the prime of their careers, and equally matched in size, strength, and technique. In spite of trying their utmost to defeat the other, the bout resulted in a draw. In spite of mastering many techniques, they had both been excellent counter-grapplers as well, so much so that the fight was virtually an ongoing array of one technique countered by another. From a critic's point of view, their bout elevated the overall image of *tegumi* wrestling. Moreover, it also provided new expectations of what was humanly possible if and when two athletes of such magnitude were pitted against each other.

Ishikawa Seijun was honorably discharged from military service and became active in the Kansai district of Japan but died during the second Sino-Japanese war. Following the war Uezu returned to Kume island where he became the principal of Kumejima High School. However, before he passed away at the age of eighty-one he was responsible for several other important undertakings which continued to distinguish his great name.

While Okinawan wrestling during the post-war era may have improved substantially, the level of wrestling demonstrated by Uezu and Ishikawa remains unique in the annals of the tradition. Perhaps one reason for this might be the subsequent development of various weight divisions. In spite of Uezu and Ishikawa's weight being much lighter than the present lightweight division, they both often fought and defeated much heavier opponents. How were such feats constantly possible for men so light in weight?

Echoing the words of Kano Jigoro when comparing modern judo to the *randori* of his art, Kushi Jokei maintained that wrestlers nowadays do not possess the technical skill once practiced, but depend more on strength and power. I agree with his analysis. Few if any develop *machi-waza*. If a small wrestler wants to defeat a larger one he must be able to secure a position tight on the opponent's hips rather than depend on *nushi-waza*. *Nushi-waza* requires wrestlers to seize each other's belt with both hands. That can, and usually is, hazardous for a small contestant when fighting a larger opponent.

Machi-waza is a technique in which a wrestler overcomes his opponent by hooking a leg behind that of his rival's. Preventing one leg from supporting the other, the attacker tightens his grip on the rival's waist and throws him to the ground on his back, ending the match. It is a difficult technique, and one that, if performed incorrectly, can have the opposite effect. In modern Okinawan sumo tournaments wrestlers fighting in even weight divisions rarely if ever attempt such a technique. However, it is thrilling to see a small competitor take out a larger one using such a tenacious strategy.

It is true that the development of weight divisions has revolutionized the native Okinawan wrestling tradition of *tegumi*. In fact, this inclusion may very well be a rational demand during an age so dominated by commercial exploitation. However, I wonder what might happen to the discipline if weight divisions were to be eliminated altogether? Would there be a resurgence of classical grappling? Would the athletes of today be forced to cultivate their technique like those who walked before them . . . the stalwarts of old-style Okinawan *tegumi*?

It wasn't until March of 1946 that the Okinawan Institute of Physical Fitness was reconstructed. By autumn of that year, sporting events like baseball, volleyball, track and field, and Okinawan sumo were successfully promoted in Ishikawa and Gushikawa. That marked an important milestone for Okinawan sumo as it was the first post-war tournament held. However, with no private transportation, both contestants and spectators had to rely on pick-up trucks and military vehicles, which were organized by the Department of Transportation.

The tournament was nearly cancelled for that reason. The organizers required thirty trucks in all but made do with far less when the government refused to provide extra assistance, citing traffic congestion as a potential hazard to emergency vehicles.

A well kept and cared for sumo practice arena in Kumoji.

Widespread devastation left most people with nothing after the war, let alone their grappling costumes for Okinawan wrestling. Hence, secondhand costumes or surplus HBT military jackets provided by the U.S. Army aptly served as competitive attire during that brief time. Additionally, promoters were also able to raise prizes from the allied forces for their tournaments.

In 1948 the third Annual Okinawan Sumo Championships, sponsored by Uruma Newspaper Company, were held at Makishiugan. As usual, the excitement of the fans rippled through the air as a memorable event took place. Itoman took top honors in team competition, followed by Chinen, with Koza finishing third. In individual competition, Nishime Noboru of Chinen walked away with first place, second went to Gaja Shosei of Naha, and Ikei Ri of Maehara finished third. Tournament participants were as follows:

Representing Itoman	Representing Koza	Representing Maehara
Akamine Shojitsu	Takara Chokichi	Nakasone Matsu
Matsuda	Kinjo Kinsei	Minei Seishin
Yoshinaga Anjun	Aniya Kenshin	Tamaki Tokuko
Nishime Hidemoto	Taira Keiichiro	Ikei Ri

Representing	Representing	Representing
Chinen	Naha	Taira
Ikeda Kosei	Gaja Shosei	Nakasone Jiro
Shinzato Eiji	Kamiya Kajun	Takashi An'ei
Ogido Seijun	Higa Shusei	Takushi Ansho
Nishime Noboru	Matayoshi Kyuzen	Shima Jokichi

The Second All Island Sumo Championships were held on October 20, 1949. Sanctioned by the Institution of Physical Fitness, and sponsored by the Uruma Newspaper Company, the tournament was held at Makishiugan. A complete success, the event included both group and individual competition and listed five groups and sixteen individual wrestlers.

The five districts included Taira, Ishikawa, Maehara, Koza, Naha, and Itoman (who were actually from Kumejima). The principal referees were Ishihara Shoutei, Kinjo Masayuki, Higa Minoru, Kushi Jokei, and Hamakawa Chiko. Additionally, each team provided one referee for the team fights. The tournament resulted in Tamaki Tokuko taking first place in individual competition, with Toguchi Eiten placing second and Kohagura Kichiichi finishing third. In the team competition it was the Itoman (Kumejima) team which took top honors, with Taira placing second, and Ishikawa finishing a respectable third.

KUSHI JOKEI: SUMO CRITIC

Kushino Taro was the pen-name used by Kushi Jokei when he wrote his commentary titled "Post-War Sumo in Okinawa" in the April 1950 edition of the *Uruma Shunju* monthly magazine. He wrote:

"Sumo in post-war Okinawa seems to lack in technique when compared to wrestling before the war. However, there can be no question that the attitude of the athletes has greatly improved. For example, among wrestlers on the circuit today there is Tamaki Tokuko of Motobu whose power is outstanding and technique distinctive. Okuma Keiko of Kinoza is also strong. In spite of being a little overweight he is still young. I believe that Okuma and Tamaki will make a great match. In spite of being very cautious, Ikei of Maehara's tenacity is beyond compare. Nishime of Chinen appeared a little weak recently. I wonder if it had something to do with too much *sake?* However, his technique remains sharp, no doubt the remnants of his previous martial arts training and experience in the navy. He is unquestionably powerful with a great fighting attitude. Fukuchi Yuji, now in Yaeyama, but once the representative for Chinen, is unsurpassed by any wrestler there. Other remarkable grapplers include Kushigen Toraichi, Shima Tsunekichi, and Kudaka Hideo."

I maintain that when compared to pre-war *tegumi*, athletes nowadays have fewer techniques and counters. For example, most wrestlers fight one-sided and don't often attempt techniques on the other side. Continuous technique and countering are rarely if ever seen. *Machiwaza* has nearly vanished altogether, and there is far too much holding.

MAKISHIUGAN: THE BIG VENUE

The tournament at Naminoue was by far the biggest event among the annual top three championships during pre-war Okinawa. However, that changed in the post-war period due largely in part to the reconstruction of the old downtown center of Naha being delayed by the development of the U.S. military bases. Business carried on in spite of the delay in reconstruction and it was during that time that commerce gradually shifted to the Makishi and Tsuboya districts.

When the All Island Sumo Tournament was held in Makishiugan a seed was planted from which a new center for sumo wrestling blossomed. Because I was the president of the Institution of Physical Fitness in Naha, as well as a city councilman, I petitioned the Mayor's office to provide a budget for the expansion of Makishiugan and the establishment of a permanent sumo ring and was successful. Hence, Makishiugan became the main venue for Okinawan sumo wrestling after the war.

As with the development of the new venue and growing popularity of Okinawan sumo, its rules and regulations were in need of revision. The escalating corruption in post-war Okinawa took its toll on sumo wrestling as well. Bouts were being rigged, there was no standard uniform, and the attitude of the athletes diminished.

As with the development and promotion of other sports, which all used a fixed standard, so too did the Okinawan Sumo Association step in and resolve the problems of the sumo community. Moreover, the old Chinese ideograms representing sumo were replaced with modern characters in an effort to enhance its image.

In 1956, the standard weight divisions of Okinawan sumo wrestling were established by Kinjo Masayuki, the association's first president, and Kushi Jokei. That improved both the quality of fighting and quantity of tournaments when compared to pre-war sumo. The annual Naminoue festival, which had been terminated because of the war, was also successfully reintroduced.

Following the term of Kinjo Masayuki as president of the association, several other prominent authorities succeeded him. They included Kushi Jokei, Akamine Kaei, Tamanaha Seikoo, Ganaha Seikichi, and Machida Soko, who was the president during the writing of this book.

In 1974, the first Japan vs. Korea Sumo Tournament was held at the Marine Exposition in Korea. Sumo wrestling in Korea is pronounced *shimuru.* Following the success of that tournament, both countries agreed to pursue an annual friendship event with each other. In November of 1977, in an effort to unify the discipline, the Okinawan Sumo Association joined forces with the Edo-Zumo

A goodwill sumo demonstration held in Korea between Japan and Korea.

Organization. Administrators concerned with the future direction of Okinawan sumo independently formed the Okinawan Sumo Institution and Mr. Gajana was selected to be its first president.

Brazil sponsored the first Okinawan World Sumo Championships in 1978. In conjunction with the seventy year anniversary of Okinawans emigrating to Brazil, five countries including Brazil, Bolivia, Japan (Okinawa), Argentina, and Peru competed for top honors. It was the first international tournament in the history of Okinawan sumo. Later, in 1981, in conjunction with the seventy-five year anniversary of Okinawan emigration to Peru, the Second World Sumo Championships were held, with the participation of five

Brazil immigration tenth anniversary tournament.

countries. In both the First and the Second World Championships, Okinawa walked away with top honors.

Marking a milestone in the annals of this exciting discipline, Okinawan sumo, a cultural tradition, has finally been introduced into the curriculum of physical education for elementary schools throughout the island. With its rise in popularity, so too has Japanese sumo wrestling begun to grow more popular in Okinawa.

Historical tablet of sumo rankings with the names of famous sumo wrestlers of Okinawa.

Establishing the friendship tournaments with foreign countries has certainly been an invaluable tool in closing the enormous distance which separates Okinawa from the rest of the world. In that regard, Okinawan sumo wrestling continues to serve as an effective international tool bridging the cultures of foreign countries. We expect to continue to develop this important socio-cultural endeavor in an effort to use sport-diplomacy as a mechanism for worldwide peace.

Statistics show that the physical fitness levels of young people nowadays has dropped radically, especially when compared to previous generations. The well-being of tomorrow's children rests in our hands today. In understanding this grave situation, I believe that by vigorously cultivating traditional athletic disciplines in local areas we would be providing the necessary foundation on which to build a stronger and wiser future generation. Like authentic karate-do, so too can Okinawan sumo wrestling be practiced anywhere, at any time, by anyone. Okinawan-style grappling is a great cultural activity for physical fitness, character development, and family togetherness.

1. According to Nagamine Sensei, folk dances which depicted combative skills during village festivals in old Okinawa were called *meikata*.

2. The Itosu family are descendants of the Baa clan.

3. The popularity of *to-te* (karate) became a more widespread practice because the physical conditioning and nature of the discipline might serve to better enhance military effectiveness.

4. Translation by Patrick McCarthy.

5. In preparation for Kano Jigoro's (the founder of judo) monumental visit to Okinawa in January of 1927, a demonstration of karate was scheduled. Among others, the presentation featured Mabuni Kenwa, Miyagi Chojun, and Kyan Chotoku. Prefectural administrators, seeking to present the to-te (Chinese martial arts) in a way which might more closely reflect its local cultivation rather than revealing its actual foreign origins, established the new terms Shuri-te, Naha-te, and Tomari-te: "te" disciplines native to Shuri, Naha, and Tomari.

6. *Toon* is pronounced "toe-on," and is actually an alternative way of pronouncing Higaonna's name.

7. A *haiku* is a traditional epigrammatic Japanese poem based on seventeen syllables; 5-7-5.

8. An English translation of that ancient text by this translator is available from Tuttle Publishing.

9. *Chuan fa* is the Chinese way of saying *kenpo*; "fist way" in English. *Chuan fa* is the correct way to describe what is often mistakenly called *kung-fu*.

10. *Kakedameshi* might better be described as a very aggressive version of *taiji* pushing hands where two opponents try virtually to knock each other down by interlocking their arms and manipulating various

techniques. *Kakedameshi,* which also employed kicking, elbow, and kneeing techniques, became quite a popular practice when seeking to determine strength or superiority in the early days of karate training in Okinawa.

11. Often people of some distinction had a prefix attached to their name to help identify them: Yamane no Chinen; Mr. Chinen from the base of the mountain district.

12. The *Bubishi,* an ancient Chinese text regarded as the "Bible of Karate," contains the history, philosophy, and application of the original self-defense traditions on which modern karate ascended. It has been translated into English and widely disseminated in the Western world by Patrick McCarthy in an edition published by Tuttle Publishing.

13. *Koshi* and *hara* both refer to the lower abdomen, hips, lower back, and buttocks functioning as a unit. *Koshi* emphasizes the physical body and *hara* has more spiritual significance.

14. *Tegumi* is the root word from which comes the word *kumite.*

15. The term *"meijin"* refers to one who has surpassed the physical boundaries of their discipline.

16. *Migiyotsu,* a sumo technique in which both wrestlers take an underarm grip on their opponent's belt with the right hand and an overarm grip with the left.

OKINAWAN KARATE AND WORLD PEACE

by Shoshin Nagamine

translated by Hideyuki Takahashi

In December 1996, Nagamine Sensei traveled to Hawaii to receive acknowledgment of his Zen realization—*Ken Zen Ichinyo* (Karate and Zen in Oneness) from the Archbishop of Daihonzan Chozen-ji, Tanouye Rotaishi, the 84th Dharma Successor of Rinzai Zen. The following is his speech given at a Testimonial Dinner held in his honor for his commitment to world peace through the Way of Karate.

INTRODUCTION

Karate is a martial art born and raised in an isolated island chain in the Pacific—Okinawa. Its marvelous trait has been widely recognized and has established worldwide popularity. Today it is also widely acknowledged that Okinawa is the main breeding ground of karate-do.

It is a well-known fact that Okinawa's karate culture has expanded all over the world. The schools of Shorin-ryu karate have established branch dojos in such various places as India, Germany, the United Kingdom and Australia. Other schools of karate have also established their own branch dojos in similar locations. As such, in terms of numbers, karate has grown to an extent we had never expected.

Karate-do is a culture of hand-to-hand fighting sprung from a technique of fist fighting. Every country has its own art of hand-to-hand fighting, which is based on the human nature of self defense and survival of the species. The art of hand to hand fighting can be categorized into two types based on the traits and cultural standard of the people of each country. The first type is the one sublimated into sports. The second type is martial arts (*budo*) which includes the development of virtue.

Karate-do is definitely a martial way, and its identity lies in *do* or principles. Any martial art without proper training of the mind turns into beastly behavior. Martial way training is a process to put forth effort to reach an eventual stage of "emptiness." What you attain through this training is called *butoku* (principles of warriors).

I cannot help thinking that postwar martial arts in Japan, possibly because of the influence of occupation policies, have turned into just martial technique and have lost their substance. Martial art students tend to be overly concerned with wins and losses and only seek reputation and awards. I am truly concerned with the fact that we have forgotten the way of mind—*shin-zen-bi* (truth, honesty, and beauty) and have lost the essence of the martial way.

In recognizing the contemporary trend, and because Okinawa is considered the Mecca of karate-do, I would like to take advantage of this opportunity to discuss the origin of Okinawa karate in reference to the history of Okinawa, its legends as well as its traditional folk songs and proverbs.

I truly believe that it is the duty of Okinawa karate people to adapt the principle of *shin-gi-tai-ichinyo*, (oneness of mind-technique-body), to the modern world, to pursue the traditional spirit of *shin-zen-bi* (truth, honesty, and beauty), and to proudly transfer karate-do to future generations.

KOKORO (SPIRIT) OF OKINAWA (RYUKYU)

Mr. Kazuo Tatsuo, an editor of *Asahi Shimbun* newspaper, has an essay titled "Ryukyu Islands." In this essay, he states:

> I had a chance to ask Mr. Shuncho Hiki, an excellent historian from Okinawa, what is the Kokoro or spirit of Okinawa (Ryukyu). Mr. Hiki responded that it was *guchoku*, or being simple and pure. Mr. Hiki further explained that Okinawans are simple and pure but have deep inner strength. Because of this, they have difficulty in changing or adapting to circumstances. Mr. Hiki added "I have lived for over 90 years. I have not been good at adapting to circumstances, because of which I have incurred losses. However, I feel this is acceptable for me."

In Okinawa, there is a saying, "your mind does not get disturbed by being beaten up, but by (you) beating up others." Simply speaking, it means that Okinawans prefer or accept the life style of being tricked and being taken advantage of, rather than hurting other people or playing tricks on them. This saying expresses the typical Okinawan spirit of being simple and pure. The idea of being simple is not the thought of those controlling or governing other people; or those who cunningly adapt to circumstances to be controlled; or of subjects just giving into the fate of being governed.

I believe the *kokoro* or spirit of Okinawa is one which shows an extreme non-resisting resistance action, beyond our imagination, when someone is cornered and/or when standing up against injustice.

WHAT WAS BROUGHT ABOUT FROM BANNING WEAPONS

Shoshin-O was enthroned at the age of thirteen. He, a believer in Buddhism, had many temples built in various areas. He stripped the local lords of weapons such as swords and spears and had them put away in warehouses inside Shuri Castle. He then declared that weapons should be used only to defend the nation and forbade the people from using any weapons for personal struggles. Moreover, he relocated the local lords to Shuri Castle and had them appointed as representatives to govern their territory. This was the way Shoshin-O eliminated the possibilities of fighting and stripped the lords of any means of revolting.

The Chusan Kingdom, thanks to the wisdom of Shoshin-O, was able to enjoy peaceful years until the invasion by Satsuma in 1609. It was a well-known story that Napoleon could not help exclaiming "What? How could such peaceful islands exist in this world without any weapons!" when he was informed of the Ryukyu Islands by a visiting British naval officer.

It is ironic that the people of this peaceful island, not having any weapons, were put under a hellish misery by the ruling Satsuma. Ryukyu people, under the tyrannical governance of Satsuma, bearing the mind-set of being simple and pure, eventually expressed an extreme action of rejection, and created te (karate), and various other splendid cultural arts through the spirit of non-resisting resistance. History indicates that people of Ryukyu have developed, without holding arms, an honorable and peaceful kingdom and culture for over 300 years.

VIEW OF DEATH BY THE RYUKYU PEOPLE — ITS DIFFERENCE FROM THOSE OF JAPANESE CULTURE

There once existed a custom of attendants setting themselves on fire following the death of their master. This custom was stopped by Shoshin-O, who forbade people from committing immolation approximately 500 years ago in 1477. One day, Shoshin-O, who had just lost his mother, was deep in sorrow. He noticed a boy crying out loud. After inquiring the reason from the boy, he was informed that the boy had been ordered to immolate himself. The boy said, "My mother does not know that I was ordered to immolate myself. How deeply saddened she will be when she finds out that I am dead!" Deeply disturbed by the severe fate of being immolated and sympathizing with the depressed feeling of the boy, Shoshin-O decided to ban immolation. This historical episode reveals how much the Ryukyu people respected life.

There is a Ryukyu chant which reads:

"In a world full of conflict and strife, do not cry over the condition of the world, your life is the treasure."

This chant, composed by well-known Ryukyu artist Yamazato Nagayoshi, was written to describe the feeling of Shotai-O, the last king of Ryukyu, as he was evacuating his castle. Ryukyu people sublimed their respect of life, beginning with the ban on immolation, up to the stage of reverence.

A Ryukyu proverb describing the mind of a Ryukyu warrior says, "even if you lose your glory, you should never give up your life." In other words, this proverb means that even if you lose your class or rank because of a new regime, you should not waste your life but try your best to survive the worst and then stand up again.

The most precious treasure in this world is your life. It is because without your life, you cannot accomplish anything.

The order banning immolation was issued by the Edo Bakufu government in 1663. Let me discuss the viewpoint towards life from the Japanese *bushido* (*Yamato Damashi-Spirit*).

Miyamoto Musashi is a well known sword master. He was a master who, through training of Japanese swordsmanship, comprehended and mastered philosophy, religion, values and arts. He left a book titled *Gorin-No-Sho* (*Book of Five Rings*) to his followers. A distillation of Musashi's ideas was contained in *Doku-Ko-Do*, (*Principles of Going Alone*). *Doku-Ko-Do* consisted of 21 articles, which he drafted to give to one of his senior disciples, Terao Magonojyo, on May 12, 1654. In Article 20, he wrote *Mi o sutetemo myori wa sutezu*—"Even though you may have to sacrifice yourself, you should not throw away your honor." In other words, he meant that if and when you disregard your honor, you are failing to follow do, principles, and gi, justice. In short, we should try to defend our honor even though we may need to sacrifice our life.

I would like to talk about *Hagakure Bushido, Hagakure Principles of the Samurai or Japanese Warrior*. Yamamoto Tsunetomo, the sage narrator of *Hagakure*, was born at the castle town of Saga in 1659 and died at the age of 61 in 1719. *Hagakure*, a dictation of his philosophy, was published in 1716. *Hagakure* was adopted as a sole textbook to instruct *bushido* to the samurai of the Saga clan. The spirit of *Hagakure* is summarized in the following four oaths:

In bushido, never be left behind.
Always be ready to serve your master.
Be dutiful to your parents.
Be merciful at all times and assist other people.

The *Hagakure* stated that if you pray these four oaths to Buddha and the Heavens every morning, then you will be able to receive their energy.

The Japanese military, who led the Japanese people into World War II, claimed that it was a sacred war not only to the Japanese but to the world and emphasized the essence of *Hagakure Bushido* as "always be ready to die." They claimed that *Hagakure* was the same as the military way of thinking, taking the lives of soldiers very lightly and leading millions of people to perish.

In the postwar era of Japan, we are in the wave of Kokusai-ka or internationalization. The people of the world are more interested in knowing the traditional culture of Japan which has been the fundamental basis of the Japanese economic growth. However, many of the Japanese are not confident enough to explain our culture to outsiders. Taking advantage of strength in the Japanese economy, more than ten million Japanese are visiting abroad and having opportunities to meet many foreign people. I am very concerned that the foreigners will form a misunderstanding that the Japanese culture is economically based and consists of only people with money.

In the historical perspective, a key factor of a nation being able to enjoy a healthy growth has been to maintain culture in one hand and martial arts in the other hand. That is, maintaining both of the above was critical in governing a nation.

True *bushido* could be explained in the following saying, "the best victory is the one attained without a battle." A group of us were deeply concerned that in the postwar era this supreme spirit has been lost. In 1993, we decided to establish *Butoku Gakkai* (Warriors' Virtue Association) under the leadership of Mr. Saburo Ishimoto, President of Chuo-Gakuin, and several other prominent people. At the beginning of our charter, it is declared that:

162

Martial arts and virtue must be unified as one.
Martial arts without virtue is simply violence.
Martial arts with virtue will purify society and culture shall flourish.

Karate master Matsumura Sokon, who was born in Shuri, Ryukyu, in 1809, taught three consecutive kings seven virtues to serve as guidelines for karate, which contributed to the maintenance of Ryukyu as a peaceful kingdom.

We, the people of Ryukyu, have learned the importance of human life through the banning of immolation. We also have learned human piety from the governance of religion and politics together. Moreover, we have created a spirit of mutual assistance. Through these lessons, island people, in peace without any weapons, have formulated an unprecedented and incomparable philosophy of *karate ni sente nashi* or "fist that does not strike first."

> *Translator's note:* Literally translated *karate ni sente nashi* says "fist that does not strike first" or "not hitting first." A deeper extension of the translation is "the fists that give life." As written in Nagamine Sensei's *Okinawa no Karate-Do*: "As a *karate-ka*, the *kokoro* (spirit/mind) of *shin-gi-tai* (mind-technique-body) is attained through spiritual forging in *zazen*. When oneness of the three, *shin-gi-tai*, is attained through spiritual forging, a true *katsu jin ken* (the fist of a person who gives life) emerges and for the first time one is able to win without a fight. Then one will truly understand *karate ni sente nashi*.

CONCLUSION

Ryukyu has overcome the tyranny of Satsuma which had lasted over 300 years since its invasion by adopting the extremely strong philosophy of resistance without resistance, as was described by Hiki Shuncho.

Karate, primarily a martial technique of self defense, has formulated a philosophy of *karate ni sente nashi* which still exists today. This philosophy could not be understood by the people based on the distorted interpretation of *bushido* spirit which took human life lightly. In a time when all the people but yourself are enemies, it was considered a matter of fact that you, holding swords on your side and carrying guns that were ready at all times, have to kill others to save your own life. The Pearl Harbor attack is one good example. I cannot help but admire the philosophy of *karate ni sente nashi* formulated by our predecessors whenever I see people in the world who are put in the midst of anguish because of weapons.

I truly believe that exercising the philosophy of *karate ni sente nashi* is the basis of true peace in the world. I have learned it from the history of Ryukyu in which they showed their respect toward human life and created a peaceful and wealthy kingdom of Ryukyu.

I would like to emphasize here that the Ryukyu people's resistance with respect to the issue of scaling down the size of United States armed forces in Okinawa is a good example of exercising the supreme right destined to the Ryukyu people from the Heavens. The people of Okinawa would never be pushed back even if governing people try to force the issue. In the end, the resolve of the people will surface and press the governments of Japan and the United States into a corner by forcing a popular vote by the people. I have to say that both governments should be fully aware of this. People will not be fooled by a short-term political solution.

I truly hope that the people of the world would change their mind-set of aggression and first-strike to a philosophy of *karate ni sente nashi*. It is only through this philosophy that world peace will be achieved.

PERSONAL HISTORY

1. Born on July 15, 1907, in Naha's Tomari village.
2. Graduated from the Naha Municipal Commercial School in 1928.
3. Enlisted into the Japanese Imperial Army in 1929, with the infantry regiment and was stationed in Oita. Transferred to Shantung Province, China, in April and experienced combat.
4. Became a prefectural policeman in December of 1931. During an air raid on October 10, 1944, he narrowly escaped death. After the war he resumed his position with the police department. In January of 1951, Nagamine was promoted to police superintendent and became the chief of police in Motobu. Retired in 1952.
5. In January of 1953, Nagamine built his 100-tsubo Karate dojo in the center of Naha and remained there for the balance of his life—forty-five years—dedicating himself to the transmission of Karate-do. During that time he also served as a city councilman for three terms and served as an executive for several major companies.
6. Died November 2, 1997, in Naha.

BUDO HISTORY

1. Started learning karate at the age of 17 years and became a direct student of Arakaki Ankichi by the time he was 19. From the time he was 26 years old he studied under Kyan Chotoku, and, at 31, also trained directly with the legendary Motobu Choki.
2. In 1940, at the age of 35, Nagamine Sensei received his teacher's license from Japan's prestigious Dai Nippon Butokukai.
3. In 1941, at the age of 36, a special karate-do committee was estab-

lished in Okinawa and he was elected to be a principal member during which time he created the *kata "Fukyugata Ichi."*

4. In 1956 the Okinawan Karate-do Association was established. Nagamine was elected to be its first vice-president.

5. From 1961 to 1969 he served as its president for four terms and received his karate-do *Hanshi* title. He retired his position and became a permanent adviser to the association.

6. In 1969 Master Nagamine experienced *satori* and became a disciple of Zen. He organized the Myoshinjiha Rengein Hanazono-kai and became its president.

7. In 1977, he founded the World Shorin-ryu Karate-do Association.

8. In November of 1981, he reorganized the Okinawa Prefectural Karate-do Association which became part of the All Japan Karate-do Association and served as its first president.

9. In April 1996, he accepted a lifetime appointment as a member of the Board of Advisers of the Institute of Zen Studies. Later that year, he was recognized by the Daihonzan Chozen-ji/International Zen Dojo for his realization through "Ken Zen Ichinyo" and given the dharma name Kenzan, or "Fist Mountain."

AWARDS

1. In July of 1976 he received the Distinguished Sports Service Award from *The Okinawa Times* (newspaper) company.

2. In November of 1979 he received the Distinguished Sports Service Award from Okinawa Prefectural Government.

3. In April of 1982 he received the Fifth Class Order of the Rising Sun from the Emperor of Japan.

For information on Matsubayashi-Ryu and the Nagamine tradition contact:

Master Takayoshi Nagamine
World Matsubayashi-Ryu (Shorin-Ryu) Karate-do Association
3-14-1 Kumoji
Naha City, Okinawa 900
Japan

Website: http://www.matsubayashi-ryu.com

For information on Zen and the Daihonzan Chozen-ji/
International Zen Dojo contact:

Institute of Zen Studies
3565 Kalihi Street
Honolulu, Hawaii 96819

Website: http://www.izs.org

Commemorative photograph taken on the 55th anniversary of the founding of the Matsubayashi-Ryu and the 85th birthday of author Shoshin Nagamine. Three generations are shown: Shoshin Nagamine, born July 15, 1907; Takayoshi Nagamine, born August 12, 1945; and Bunshiro Nagamine, born May 3, 1977.

Author Shoshin Nagamine (right) and son Takayoshi Nagamine (left) practicing *yakusoku kumite*. **September 1, 1991.**